MONETARY POLICY AND FINANCIAL INNOVATIONS IN FIVE INDUSTRIAL COUNTRIES

Also by Stephen F. Frowen

BUSINESS, TIME AND THOUGHT: Selected Papers of
 G. L. S. Shackle (*editor*)
CONTROLLING INDUSTRIAL ECONOMIES (*editor*)
MONETARY POLICY AND ECONOMIC ACTIVITY IN WEST GERMANY
 (*editor with A. S. Courakis and M. H. Miller*)
A FRAMEWORK OF INTERNATIONAL BANKING (*editor*)
UNKNOWLEDGE AND CHOICE IN ECONOMICS: Proceedings of the
 George Shackle Conference (*editor*)

Monetary Policy and Financial Innovations in Five Industrial Countries

The UK, the USA, West Germany, France and Japan

Edited by

Stephen F. Frowen

and

Dietmar Kath

St. Martin's Press   New York

First published in the United States of America in 1992

Printed in Great Britain

ISBN 0–312–03523–3

Library of Congress Cataloging-in-Publication Data
Frowen, Stephen F.
Monetary policy and financial innovations in five industrial
countries: UK, USA, West Germany, France, and Japan / Stephen F.
Frowen and Dietmar Kath.
p. cm.
Includes index.
ISBN 0–312–03523–3
1. Monetary policy   2. Monetary policy—United States.
3. Monetary policy—European Economic Community countries.
4. Monetary policy—Japan.   5. Money supply—European Economic
Community countries.   6. Money supply—Japan.   I. Kath, Dietmar.
II. Title.
HG230.3.F77   1992
332.4'6—dc20   90–8924
                                                                    CIP

Contents

List of Figures and Tables	vi
Notes on the Contributors	viii
Introduction	xii

1 National Monetary Policy in an Open World Economy   1
  Claus Köhler

2 Federal Reserve Policy since October 1979: A Justified
  Response to Financial Innovations?   16
  Thomas Mayer

3 The Control of Monetary Aggregates in the Federal
  Republic of Germany under Changing Conditions   32
  Norbert Kloten

4 Financial Innovations and the Stability of the Demand
  for Money in Germany since 1974   59
  Stephen F. Frowen and Heinrich Schlomann

5 The Effects of Financial Innovation and Deregulation on
  French Monetary Policy   82
  Robert Raymond

6 Monetary Control in Japan   101
  Tatsuya Tamura

7 Financial Innovation: A View from the Bank of England   120
  John S. Flemming

8 Capital Flows and Exchange Rates: Some Implications   129
  Gordon T. Pepper

9 British Monetary Policy: October 1990   142
  C. A. E. Goodhart

Name Index	161
Subject Index	163

List of Figures and Tables

Figures

3.1 West German money stock and central bank money
stock, 1975–89   35
3.2 West German money stock M3 and production
potential, 1962–88   38
3.3 West German interest rate movements, 1974–89   48
6.1 Money supply and GNP in Japan, 1956–86
(percentage change from same period of previous
year)   110

Tables

3.1 West German monetary targets and their
implementation, 1975–89   42
3A.1 Weights of West Germany's main components in
M3 and the central bank money stock (CBMS) and
their relative share (end of 1987)   56
4.1 OLS-estimation results for the West German
nominal demand for money: M1   63
4.2 OLS-estimation results for the West German real
demand for money: M1   64
4.3 OLS-estimation results for the West German
nominal demand for money: M2   66
4.4 OLS-estimation results for the West German real
demand for money: M2   67
4.5 OLS-estimation results for the West German
nominal demand for money: M3   69
4.6 OLS-estimation results for the West German real
demand for money: M3   70
4.7 OLS-estimation results for the West German
nominal demand for money from 1974 to 1980   72
4.8 OLS-estimation results for the West German real
demand for money from 1974 to 1980   73
4.9 OLS-estimation results for the West German
nominal demand for money from 1981 to 1987
(1st quarter)   74

4.10	OLS-estimation results for the West German real demand for money from 1981 to 1987 (1st quarter)	75
4.11	Results of the Chow-test for alternative estimates for West Germany: 1980 (4th quarter)	77
5.1	The shifting structure of French sectoral financial surpluses and deficits, 1979–88	83
5.2	Gross issues in the French bond market, 1972–89	86
5.3	Net bond issues/GDP in West Germany, UK, France, USA and Japan in 1985 and 1988 (%)	86 86
5.4	Distribution of gross bond issues in France, 1975–89	87
5.5	Net bond issues in France in 1984 and 1988	88
5.6	Main features of French money market securities	90
6.1	Japanese money supply forecasts, 1978–89 (in percentage changes over previous year)	105
6.2	Changes in various types of Japanese financial assets between 1980 and 1986	115
8A.1	Impact of a rise in the US budget and trade deficit	140

Notes on the Contributors

John S. Flemming is an Executive Director of the Bank of England. He was previously (1965–80) an Official Fellow in Economics and Bursar of Nuffield College, Oxford, and since 1980 has been a member of the Council and Executive Committee of the Royal Economic Society. Since 1986 he has also been a member of the Advisory Board on Research Councils. Mr Flemming was Editor of *The Economic Journal* from 1976–1980. His principal contributions cover aspects of capital theory, intertemporal decisions and decisions under uncertainty, together with some empirical and policy applications. Apart from contributions to learned journals and collective volumes, he published *Why We Need a Wealth Tax* (with M. D. Little) (1974) and *Inflation* (1976).

Stephen F. Frowen was Bundesbank Professor of Monetary Economics in the Free University of Berlin. On his return to the United Kingdom in 1989 the title of Honorary Research Fellow in the Department of Economics was conferred on him by University College London. Professor Frowen was previously Professor of Economics at the University of Frankfurt and for many years held senior teaching posts at the University of Surrey, following an appointment as Research Officer at the National Institute of Economic and Social Research. He has published extensively in monetary economics and banking and was Editor of *The Bankers' Magazine* (now *Banking World*). He has been a visiting professor in several European countries. He is the Editor of *Unknowledge and Choice in Economics* (1990), *Business, Time and Thought: Selected Papers of G. L. S. Shackle* (1988), *Controlling Industrial Economies* (1983), *A Framework of International Banking* (1979) and *Monetary Policy and Economic Activity in West Germany* (with A. S. Courakis and M. H. Miller, 1977). He is also the translator into English of Knut Wicksell's *Value, Capital and Rent* (with a foreword by G. L. S. Shackle (1954, reprinted 1970).

Charles A. E. Goodhart is the Norman Sosnow Professor of Banking and Finance at the London School of Economics. Before joining LSE in 1985, he worked at the Bank of England for seventeen years as a monetary adviser, becoming a Chief Adviser in 1980. Earlier he had taught at Cambridge and the London School of Economics, and was an Economic Adviser in the Department of Economic Affairs (1965–6). He has written a couple of books on monetary history and has recently revised his graduate monetary textbook, *Money, Information and Uncertainty* (2nd edn, 1989). He published a collection of papers on monetary policy, *Monetary Theory and Practice* (1984), and an institutional study of *The Evolution of Central Banks* (1988).

Dietmar Kath is Professor of Economics at the University of Duisburg in the Federal Republic of Germany. He graduated at the University of Hamburg in 1961, took his PhD at the University of Hamburg in 1966 and his higher doctorate at the University of Freiburg in 1974 with a study on 'The Interest Rate Structure of Financial Markets'. His main research interests in the field of monetary theory and policy include the term structure of interest rates, exchange-rate systems and balance-of-payments problems. He has published widely in these fields and is also Co-Editor and Co-author of one of the most successful German textbooks: *Economic Theory and Economic Policy*. He has been a visiting professor at the Universities of Bonn, Siegen and Passau, and since 1977 has been an elected member of the Monetary Committee of the German Society for Economic and Social Sciences.

Norbert Kloten is President of the Land Central Bank of Baden-Württemberg and an *ex officio* member of the decision-making West German Central Bank Council. He graduated at the University of Bonn and later became a Visiting Lecturer at the Johns Hopkins University (Bologna Center) in Italy. In 1960 he was appointed Professor of Economics at the University of Tübingen and was awarded an honorary degree by the University of Karlsruhe in 1980. He combined the Tübingen Chair with membership of the West German Council of Economic Experts (*Sachverständigenrat*) from 1969 to 1976, being its Chairman from 1970 to 1976. He remains Honorary Professor at the University of Tübingen and is also a member of the Board of Academic and Non-academic Associations, of the Trilateral Commission and other organisations. He has published widely on the principles of economic policy and in the field of monetary and international economics, on regional and development problems, as well as on the methodological aspects of science.

Claus Köhler is Professor of Economics and Director of the Institute for Empirical Economic Research in Berlin. He was an Executive Director of the Deutsche Bundesbank and a member of the Central Bank Council from 1974 until he joined the Board of the Treuhandgesellschaft in October 1990. He holds degrees from the Humboldt and Free University, Berlin and began his academic career at the Technische Universität Berlin as a Lecturer in Economics. From 1966–74 he was Professor of Economics at the University of Hanover. During his earlier banking career he held leading positions with banks in Berlin and finance companies. He was a member of the German Council of Economic Experts from 1969 to 1974 and more recently has been Honorary Professor of Economics at the Universities of Hanover and Frankfurt. He has published widely in the areas of monetary economics and applied economics and is the author of *Der Geldkreislauf* (1962); *Orientierungshilfen für die Kreditpolitik* (1968); *Geldwirtschaft*, Vol. I: *Geldversorgung und Kreditpolitik*, 2nd ed. (1977); *Geldwirtschaft*, Vol. II: *Zahlungsbilanz und Wechselkurs* (1979); *Geldwirtschaft*, Vol. III: *Wirtschaftspolitische Ziele und wirtschaftspolitische Strategie* (1983); and *Internationalökonomie* (1990).

Thomas Mayer is Professor of Economics at the University of California, Davis. He was born in Vienna, Austria, in 1927 and received his PhD from Columbia University in 1953. His main fields of interest are monetary policy and applied monetary theory. He is the co-author of *Monetary Policy in the United States* (1968), *Intermediate Macroeconomics* (with D. C. Rowan, 1972), *Permanent Income, Wealth and Consumption* (1972), *The Structure of Monetarism* (with P. Cagan, B. Friedman *et al.*, 1978), *Money, Banking and the Economy* (4th edn, 1990), *Revealing Monetary Policy* (1987) and *Monetarism and Macroeconomic Policy* (1991). He also edited *The Political Economy of American Monetary Policy* (1990). He is currently working on a book on the methodology of economics.

Gordon T. Pepper, CBE, is an honorary visiting professor in the Department of Banking and Finance and director of the Midland Montagu Centre for Research in Financial Markets at the City University Business School in London. He is a member of the Economic and Social Research Council. He is also a director and senior adviser of Midland Montagu, which is the international and investment banking arm of the Midland Group. Professor Pepper was previously chairman of Greenwell Montagu & Co. and, before that, joint senior partner of W. Greenwell & Co. He was the joint founder of the gilt-edged business of W. Greenwell & Co. and the premier gilt-edged analyst in the United Kingdom from 1972 until 1981. He is a fellow of the Institute of Actuaries and the Society of Investment Analysts and earned his MA in economics from Trinity College, Cambridge.

Robert Raymond is General Manager of the Research Department (Direction Générale des Etudes) at the Bank of France. Since 1975, his main field of responsibilities has been monetary policy. After reading law and economics, he joined the Bank of France in 1951 as an inspector. Following a few years spent in banking supervision, he was seconded from the Bank of France to the Federal Reserve Bank of New York in 1966. From 1968 to 1975, he was appointed to the Foreign Department (Direction Générale des Services Etrangers) at the Bank of France. At the same time, Mr. Raymond performed several functions outside the Bank of France, notably for the French five-year plan. He has also been professor at several universities in Paris and abroad. Since 1981, he has chaired the group of monetary experts on the Committee of Governors of EEC central banks. He has written several books as well as many papers, articles and reviews in the field of monetary policy.

Heinrich Schlomann is a Research Associate of the Johann Wolfgang Goethe-Universität Frankfurt am Main, Institute of Social Policy, concerning the project 'Social Security' of the Special Collaborative Programme 3: 'Microanalytical Foundations of Social Policy'. He graduated from the University of Hanover with a major in Economics. His diploma thesis was on theoretical aspects of the demand for money and related empirical evidence for the Federal Republic of Germany. Presently he is working on his doctoral thesis on the distribution and accumulation of wealth in Germany, with special reference to precautionary savings of the elderly.

Tatsuya Tamura is Director of the Policy Planning Department of the Bank of Japan. Following a series of managerial positions, he became the Bank of Japan's Chief Representative in Europe in 1986 prior to his posts first as Director of the Bank's Government Bond Department and subsequently as Director of the Research and Statistics Department. Mr Tamura earned his BA in law from the University of Tokyo and his MA in economics from the University of Pennsylvania. In the early 1970s he was one of the co-authors of the so-called *White Paper on Japan's Economy*.

Introduction

Financial innovations have been a worldwide phenomenon since the 1970s, reaching a climax during the 1980s. The objective of the present volume is to analyse the response to these developments – closely linked with the liberalisation of money and capital markets – and the consequences for the conduct of monetary policy. Also considered is the stability of hitherto-established relationships between economic variables on which the reliability of monetary policy measures depends. The volume further covers some of the international aspects involved and the important implications of dominant and persistent flows of long-term capital across the exchanges which have emerged in recent years.

This book is the result of a conference on 'Financial Innovations, Deregulation and the Control of Monetary Aggregates' which was organised by both editors at the University of Surrey in Guildford (England). It contains most of the papers presented on that occasion, each in a revised and completely updated version. The papers by Charles A. E. Goodhart and Gordon T. Pepper included here replace those originally presented at the conference.

The macroeconomic consequences of financial innovations on individual countries diverge greatly and depend on the degree to which the institutional framework of financial centres differs. The principal concern of the conference was therefore to examine the hypothesis that under divergent institutional conditions the impact of financial innovations and deregulations on individual money and capital markets will not be homogeneous. For this purpose the financial developments in five leading industrial countries – the UK, the USA, West Germany (at that time), France and Japan – were analysed theoretically as well as empirically by professional economists and central bankers from these countries, all of whom are experts in the fields of both monetary theory and monetary policy.

There are three main topics which may be chosen for a general summary of the papers collected in this volume investigating the impact of financial innovations and deregulations:

First, the increasing instability of central monetary variables and aggregates at the domestic level;
second, the wider exchange-rate fluctuations at the international level; and

third, the reduced controlability of monetary aggregates by domestic central banks.

A finding emerging from most of the papers is that at the domestic level financial innovations lead to greater interest-rate volatility and stronger fluctuations in the velocity of circulation of the money supply. However, there are some indications in the papers by Norbert Kloten and Stephen F. Frowen and Heinrich Schlomann that this general conclusion has only limited applicability for the Federal Republic of Germany. Until the unification of the two parts of Germany in 1990, there was no conclusive evidence of shocks or structural breaks in the West German demand for money function. But, as Norbert Kloten makes clear in his paper, there was little need in West Germany for further deregulations in the financial sector, and the introduction of additional financial innovations remained at a low key.

Thomas Mayer, basing his arguments on monetary developments in the USA and within the framework of an *IS/LM* analysis, concludes that financial innovations can be interpreted as impulses on the *LM*-curve. But, as he explains, one can find arguments for a steepening as well as for a flattening of the *LM*-curve. A steeper *LM*-curve would be due to a lower, and a flatter curve due to a higher, interest elasticity of the money-demand function.

At the international level there appears to be a broad consensus with regard to the impact of financial innovations on capital movements and exchange-rate stability. The views on these issues expressed by some of the contributors could be compressed as follows:

First, international capital movements are attracted by positive interest-rate differentials;
second, as new instruments for international lending and borrowing as well as for financial investments are devised in order to utilise comparative interest-rate advantages, an expansion of international capital movements is set in motion; and
third, innovations of international financial instruments are therefore responsible for the dramatic exchange-rate fluctuations experienced since the late 1970s.

Concerning the consequences of financial innovations for monetary control and for monetary targeting, a distinction has to be made between the domestic and the world economy. Looking first at the domestic monetary policy aspects of financial innovations, it would be justified to say that monetary aggregates would tend to become less effective variables for monetary targeting. Both Thomas Mayer and Charles A. E. Goodhart raise the question whether monetary policy should perhaps be shifted to a nominal GNP-target in line with the Tobin proposal; that is, instead of using a money-supply aggregate for control purposes, the central bank should switch to a velocity-corrected monetary aggregate (M times V). Such a concept could be called the 'effective quantity of money'. Any change in money velocity should be neutralised by opposite movements in the aggregate itself, so that the product of the two remains at its target level. Both authors reject this possibility for different reasons.

With regard to the international aspects of financial innovations and their policy implications, it is argued that the strong fluctuations in exchange rates resulting therefrom offer additional problems for both domestic and international monetary policies. Claus Köhler as well as Gordon T. Pepper point out that fluctuations in exchange rates are mainly the result of speculative capital movements, i.e. capital transactions primarily induced by speculation. In other words, capital movements of this nature are in no way linked to the international flow of goods and services. Köhler therefore proposes to dampen exchange-rate fluctuations by a coordinated intervention in foreign exchange markets on the part of central banks representing the world's major international currencies. By such coordination – according to Köhler – international financial investors and those engaged in international trade would be provided with an 'anchor' for their policy decisions.

The editors would like to express their special debt of gratitude to the Goethe-Institute, London, and in particular to its former Director, Dr G. Coenen, for generous financial support for the conference. They also take this opportunity of expressing the warmest gratitude to Mr T. M. Farmiloe and Mr Keith Povey for their tremendous editorial support.

June 1991
STEPHEN F. FROWEN
*University College London and
St Edmund's College, Cambridge*

DIETMAR KATH
University of Duisburg

1 National Monetary Policy in an Open World Economy

Claus Köhler

1.1 NATIONAL ECONOMIC POLICY OBJECTIVES

Almost every country and the European Economic Community, too, wants to have stable prices in its territory and to attain appropriate economic growth and thus full employment. Many economies – industrial and developing countries alike – have succeeded in reducing their inflation rates distinctly in recent years. After the second oil price explosion at the end of the 1970s had been overcome, the rates of economic growth – also of both industrial and developing countries – settled down at around 3 per cent a year. Now, however, the expansionary forces appear to be flagging. At all events, recent economic growth has not been strong enough to solve the main problem currently facing national economies, that is, unemployment. Unemployment rates have remained high. In a number of countries – notably the United States and, to some extent, the Federal Republic of Germany – economic growth rates have exceeded the average. In those nations the unemployment rates have declined. In other countries where economic growth has been below the average, such as France and the United Kingdom, they have risen further.

No national economy is able to achieve its economic policy objectives in isolation from the rest of the world economy. All countries interchange goods and services. The international division of labour, which this reflects, is a prerequisite for economic growth in every economy. Conversely, changes in the world economy also affect economic developments in national economies. In the long run a free exchange of goods and services is possible and can be expanded only if it is accompanied by free international movements of money and capital. If one speaks of innovations in international monetary markets, this attests to a process of increasing liberalisation of international money and capital movements. A process of this kind is

1

gratifying because it can promote the exchange of goods and services and result at the same time in a reasonable distribution of financial resources. Moreover, the free exchange of goods, services, money and capital constitutes a counterbalance to protectionist trends. The more liberally international trade is structured, the sooner the threshold of pain will be reached when protectionist measures are mooted. The adverse repercussions of protectionist measures on an economy which adopts them are then likewise substantial.

National monetary policy, as part of national economic policy, must operate under the prevailing conditions of an open world economy. Even on a national scale it is obvious that monetary policy, acting on its own, can neither stabilise prices nor attain any other national economic policy objective. To manage this, monetary policy and fiscal policy must work together on the basis of an overall economic policy strategy. In addition, management and labour, in their incomes policy, must remain within the confines of an overall economic policy strategy of this kind. It goes without saying that, in an open world economy, monetary policy has even greater difficulty in achieving the national objectives set for it. Events on the monetary markets of other economies and on international monetary markets affect interest rates, liquidity and, at times, also the effectiveness of the monetary policy instruments employed in the national economy.

To produce an optimum economic policy result it is necessary, even within a national economy, for monetary and fiscal policy to work together, and for the economic policy-makers to achieve a consensus with management and labour. In an open world economy it is essential, in addition, for national economies to co-operate with one another on international goods markets and international monetary markets when problems arise.

1.2   THE EXCHANGE RATE PROBLEM

A number of European countries enjoy the advantage of being able to conduct their mutual economic activity – which includes a large part of their total international trade – at fixed exchange rates. This is made possible by the intervention mechanism within the European Monetary System (EMS). The fact that central banks are prepared to maintain a particular exchange rate level, and that they affirm this by means of interventions, stabilises exchange rate expectations. This creates a reliable basis of calculation and minimises expenditure on forward exchange cover. Under such a system one is fairly close to a state of 'monetary indifference', that is, a state in which it makes no difference to an enterprise which currency its cash balances are held in.

Fixed exchange rates, like those prescribed under the European Monetary System, cannot be maintained over the longer term if inflation rates in the countries participating in the intervention mechanism diverge. As this is the case in the EMS, it is necessary to readjust exchange rates from time to time. Such a realignment of parities is often associated with speculative transactions which disrupt national monetary policy. The interventions which are then required – sometimes on a considerable scale – may inject substantial amounts of liquid funds into the banking system, or deprive it of such funds. Nevertheless, European central banks have always succeeded to date in neutralising the liquidity inflows or outflows by means of monetary policy measures, and restoring calm to the foreign exchange markets of the affected currencies for fairly long periods of time.

Serious disruptions of global economic developments and national economic trends have been caused by freely floating exchange rates and particularly by the floating key currency, the US dollar. In recent years these exchange rates have fluctuated exceptionally sharply. For example, the rate for the dollar in terms of the Deutsche Mark declined from DM 2.82 on 19 March 1973 to DM 1.71 on 3 January 1980. That represented an average annual DM appreciation rate of 7 per cent. Up to 26 February 1985 the dollar then rose to DM 3.47, or at an average annual rate of 15 per cent. Precisely two years later, on 26 February 1987, the dollar stood at DM 1.82. That was an average annual DM appreciation rate of 28 per cent.

Exchange rate movements of this kind have a direct impact on economic developments in national economies. When exchange rates are floating freely, the liquidity effects that a central bank can neutralise are absent. Exchange rate fluctuations work through immediately to economic trends. For instance, an appreciation of the Deutsche Mark makes West German products more expensive abroad and thus dampens exports. West German firms' costs, calculated in US dollars, go up in line with the appreciation rate, which reduces their international competitiveness. In order to avoid the threatening sales losses, enterprises then invest less in their home country, whose currency is appreciating, and more in the country with the depreciating currency. Domestic capital formation is adversely affected. The appreciation makes imported goods cheaper. The imports that are flooding the domestic market replace home-produced goods. Domestic production suffers accordingly. During the late autumn 1986, at the exchange rate level of DM 2.00 to DM 2.10 per dollar ruling at the time, it was reasonable to suppose that the growth rate of real gross national product (GNP) in West Germany, at 2.5 to 3 per cent, would be stronger than that of production potential, and that unemployment would consequently go down further. At an exchange rate level of around DM 1.80, these forecasts will no doubt have to be revised distinctly downwards.

On the foreign exchange market two mutually incompatible interests are emerging: enterprises' interest in an appropriate and stable exchange rate level, and speculators' interest in exchange rate changes. It has to be conceded that monetary transactions on the international money and capital markets, and hence also on the foreign exchange market, have parted company with transactions in goods, services and investments. Hence it is the scale of speculative transactions that determines market trends. On a disoriented and leaderless foreign exchange market, this results in the swings in exchange rates which we have witnessed. Enterprises can do nothing about this. They must cover themselves against exchange risks as best as they can.

The depreciation of the US dollar is sometimes also seen as an instrument for reducing current account balances, and particularly the massive current account deficit being run by the United States. Hence attempts have been made, with the aid of an 'open-mouth policy', to keep the depreciation going. This, however, is an approach which is apt to pose problems. In the light of the experience gained in the 1930s, when countries vied with one another in devaluing their currencies, it was decided that exchange rates should not be used any more as instruments of economic policy. The pace of the recent depreciation of the dollar likewise gives cause for concern. The immediate outcome has been a steep rise in the cost of US imports and a sharp fall in the cost of European imports. The likely volume effect of falling imports to the United States and rising imports to Europe takes time to make itself felt compared with the price effect. Owing to this *J*-curve impact, the marked depreciation of the US dollar is leading to no, or only an inadequate, reduction in the nominal current account balances. Hence the depreciation of the dollar may well be going further than would be necessary to adjust the current account over the medium term.

The exchange rate is apparently also being used as an economic

policy instrument by a number of (mostly heavily indebted) developing countries. Given the galloping inflation rampant in these countries, constant devaluations against the US dollar are required. In the
process these countries are endeavouring to devalue their own currency more than would be consistent with the difference between
their respective inflation rates. This real devaluation is intended to
boost their exports. On the other hand, it makes the repayment of
their foreign debt more difficult, since a larger amount of domestic
currency is needed to discharge that debt. This larger amount can in
fact be earned if sales can be stepped up in real terms. This, however,
is difficult to do. There remains the option of raising the prices of
domestic products. But this aggravates inflation. This, too, shows
how two-edged the exchange rate is when used as an economic policy
instrument.

National monetary policy-makers cannot ignore these developments on the foreign exchange markets. As their interest rate and
liquidity policy measures affect exchange rates too, they have to take
into account the impact on prices, business activity, current account
balances and the debt problem. Speculative inflows resulting from
expectations of exchange rate appreciation may cause monetary
aggregates to grow regardless of whether a central bank intervenes or
exchange rates fall. To reverse such rises in the money stock, interest
rates must be lowered to allow the funds to drain off abroad from the
domestic market. In other words, the monetary policy measures
required are different from – and sometimes diametrically opposed to
– those needed when the money stock is increasing as a result of
mounting economic activity. Monetary expansions of the latter kind
would have to be countered by raising interest rates.

1.3   THE CURRENT ACCOUNT PROBLEM

It is difficult to assess up to what point current account balances are
tolerable. The bounds are set in practice by the size of the monetary
reserves which a country can use to finance its current account
deficits, and by a country's capacity to borrow abroad. Since both are
limited the tolerable current account deficits, and hence current
account surpluses, are likewise limited. The US current account
deficit and the Japanese and West German current account surpluses
are all regarded as being too high.

There is a domestic facet to this as well. The USA will reduce its current account deficit only if the growth rate of GNP is higher than that of domestic demand. In other words, domestic expenditure must lag behind total value added in order to make room for exports. If this happens without any economic growth, or at only a low growth rate, then domestic demand must be dampened. This is a painful process, and difficult to implement politically. In 1987 the United States wanted to reach a 3 per cent growth rate in real GNP, while holding down the rise in public expenditure to 1 per cent. In order to reduce the public sector and current account deficits in Japan and the Federal Republic of Germany, by contrast, domestic demand must increase faster than GNP. In West Germany this did indeed happen in 1986, and it is the target for future years as well. Monetary policy is also involved in wrestling with these problems.

In addition, there is an international facet to the current account problem. Countries running current account surpluses lend to non-residents, and countries running current account deficits borrow from non-residents. This gives rise to the proposition: industrial countries must run current account surpluses. They must lend to developing countries so that the latter can afford a current account deficit. Such deficits are necessary to enable developing countries to import the goods they need for their economic growth. Today, however, the problem facing many developing countries is that they have to repay credit. To make this easier for them, all industrial countries taken together should run a balance-of-payments deficit as, indeed, is currently the case. If it is wished to help developing countries here and to enable them to import additional products, then they must be given additional opportunities of exporting goods. This in turn means that the markets of industrial countries must be kept open for products from developing countries, and that the growth rate of GNP in industrial countries must be relatively high. These problems likewise have a bearing on national monetary policy.

1.4   THE DEBT PROBLEM

The debt problem, that is, the problem that a number of countries are finding it difficult to pay the interest and repay the principal on debts they have incurred, is the outcome of an overly strong credit expansion on the international monetary markets. During the period from 1972 to 1981 the external lending of banks in the member countries of the International Monetary Fund (IMF) rose from US

$264 billion to US $2138 billion, or at an average annual growth rate of 26 per cent. During that period fierce competition apparently prevented the self-regulation of this massive credit expansion. The process did not come to a halt until the insolvency of a number of countries was manifest.

Such a prolonged sharp credit expansion is hardly conceivable in traditional countries. Monetary policy and bank supervision set basic conditions which prevent the provision of funds from getting out of hand. Many banks have therefore started operations in offshore centres, those in Europe in Luxembourg, those in USA in the Bahamas, the Cayman Islands, the Netherlands Antilles and Panama, and those in Asia in Bahrain, Hong Kong and Singapore. In these offshore centres there is often no real central bank and thus no monetary policy control. Bank supervision is frequently more lenient than in the traditional economies. In other words, the scope for extending credit is relatively wide in offshore centres. To cite an example, at the beginning of the strong expansion on the international credit markets in 1972, the ratio of the foreign lending of all banks in Luxembourg to the foreign lending of West German banks was 62 per cent. By the end of the strong credit expansion in 1981 this figure had risen to 134 per cent. Efforts by a number of central banks, including the Deutsche Bundesbank, to damp down this explosion by introducing European minimum reserve requirements, or a prudential ratio linking the volume of foreign lending to a bank's liable capital, proved to be unworkable.

When banks begin operations in offshore centres, they are faced with a funding problem. For the most part they only have access to money-market funds, while on the other hand they have to meet a demand for medium- and long-term credit. An innovation was helpful here: the roll-over technique. Banks engaged in excessive maturity transformation by raising funds at short term and granting medium- and long-term loans. They passed on the resultant risk to borrowers, who had to pay interest rates that were linked to the refinancing costs. It was apparently completely overlooked that a risk does not vanish if it is foisted on to someone else. This became plain when money-market rates (six-month LIBOR – London interbank offered rate) – which had stood at 6 per cent at the beginning of the expansionary process – rose to double-digit levels, running at between 16 and 17 per cent in 1981. Borrowers were unable to pay such high rates. The maturity transformation risk which the banks had passed on recoiled on them as a creditworthiness risk.

In the meantime the entire world economy, as well as economic policy, and thus also monetary policy – indeed, it is fair to say, politics in general – are feeling the effects of this debt problem. The problem can be solved, economically speaking, if the debtor countries succeed in gradually growing into their overly large 'debt cloak'. This is in fact the basic idea behind the Baker Plan of sustained growth. The US Treasury Secretary is trying to achieve such growth by calling upon the debtor countries, the international financing institutions – particularly the World Bank and the IMF – and the creditor banks, to collaborate to ensure growth of this kind.

Whether this strategy can be implemented, and how effective it proves to be, will depend upon many factors. Three influences will be of particular importance: international commodity prices, the volume of world trade and the level of interest rates on international monetary markets. For many of the debtor countries international commodity prices are the prices of their exports. These prices have gone down steadily throughout the 1980s right up to the present, and are now running at about 70 per cent of their 1980 level. Economic policies have no effect on this trend. The export potential of many debtor countries is determined by the growth rate of world trade. For 1992 this rate has been estimated at 6 per cent, provided that the original assumptions about economic growth in the United States, Europe and Japan prove correct. Given the marked depreciation of the dollar against the currencies of the United States' trading partners, however, this now appears doubtful. So the only variable that can still be influenced by economic policy is the interest-rate level. The fact that interest rates in the United States, and thus also on international monetary markets, declined in 1987 – 6-month LIBOR was down to 6 per cent – owed a good deal to the debt problem.

National monetary policy in other countries is also being affected by that problem. The deficit on the US current account can be offset by other countries 'voluntarily' investing funds of their own in the United States. Given the ruling exchange rates, the US demand for foreign capital should then be matched by a corresponding supply. Failing this, the US current account would be adjusted via exchange rate arbitrage. That implies a further depreciation of the US dollar. If this is to be prevented, and if the 'voluntary' approach is to be encouraged, interest rates in Europe and Japan must be lower than those in the United States. Only if there is an appropriate interest rate differential will Europeans and Japanese look for financial investments in the USA. It is quite conceivable that this will put monetary policy in Europe and Japan in a dilemma between various aspects of economic activity. It is at this point that it becomes evident how closely monetary policy is involved in overall economic developments, that is, in domestic problems as well as in the current account problem, the debt problem and the exchange rate problem.

1.5 THE EXPANSION ON THE INTERNATIONAL BOND MARKETS

In 1981 the expansion on the international credit market gave way to an expansion on the international bond market. Since then the issue volume has risen year by year at an average annual rate of 33 per cent. A rate of this kind – which masks issue volumes of US $40 billion in 1980, and US $226 billion in 1986 – indicates that these financial transactions have likewise parted company with activities in the goods, services, and investment sectors and have become independent to some extent. The risks are growing at a disproportionately fast pace on this market too.

One would suppose that it is not possible for excessive issuing activity on a bond market to go on for over six years. The self-regulation process should intervene, if only because there can hardly be such a large number of issuers. Actual practice shows, however, that issuers who are not triple A – that is, who do not really belong there at all – also enter this market. Issuers are lured into launching bonds on the market by means of additional profits. These enterprises add to their portfolios previously issued bonds which offer an interest rate gain relative to their own issues. Many issues come into being because the amount of the issue is converted into a different currency (likewise with a profit for the issuer).

Investors should be another retarding factor that might result in self-regulation. They, too, can scarcely be expected to buy issue amounts that are constantly rising so steeply. But this curb has also proved ineffective up to now. This is because issuers often garnish their securities with speculative trimmings which offer buyers, besides the relatively low interest rate (which in turn attracts issuers), prospects of speculative profits. In the light of the prevailing interest and exchange rate expectations, the market is constantly spawning innovations. Thanks to these speculative incentives, sufficient investors have always been forthcoming to date and have bought up the bonds issued.

National monetary policy is also affected by developments on the international bond market. Depending on interest and exchange rate expectations, a central bank must count on securities being offered or sought on a major scale on its national capital market. The consequence is that fluctuations in yields on the bond market are greater than they used to be. Owing to the speculative behaviour of many security holders on the bond market, interest-rate policy measures by a central bank may have different effects from those produced in the past. For example, if the Bundesbank lowers money market rates, the market expects the Deutsche Mark (DM) to depreciate. As a result it disposes of DM paper, bond prices fall and yields rise. Hence, when selecting its monetary policy instruments, a central bank must pay greater heed than in the past to the impact its measures might have on expectations and on consequent decisions. As far as possible, therefore, the Bundesbank changes money-market rates with the aid of open market operations, rather than by raising or lowering the discount and lombard rates, the latter being the rate charged for Bundesbank advances covered by eligible bills of exchange and other securities. This is because the 'signal effect' of changes in key interest rates, and hence the impact on exchange rate expectations, is substantial.

1.6 THE PROBLEM OF MONOCAUSALITY

A national monetary policy which seeks to contribute successfully in its country to price stability, and which is designed to help achieve appropriate economic growth and full employment, must pay due regard to numerous domestic and external influences. It is no good at all singling out particular factors and thus trying to account for economic developments monocausally, and to base measures of economic policy, and hence also of monetary policy, on such mono-causal connections.

The only advantage of a monocausal approach is that analysis and therapy sound simple, and therefore – more's the pity – often also convincing: too much money leads to price rises. The central bank can control the money stock and consequently is responsible for price stability. The difference in inflation rates between two countries, that is the change in purchasing power parity, determines exchange rate movements. Speculation on the foreign exchange market has a stabilising effect. All these statements take account of only one aspect of the whole in both analysis and therapy. But in reality conditions are determined, not by just one factor at a time, but by many simultaneously.

The statement that too much money leads to price rises is correct when in an upswing much credit is requested and granted, and the monetary aggregates increase accordingly. Such a process reflects an expansion of demand which will lead sooner or later to price rises. However, it is also possible for the money stock to grow without price rises ensuing. When at the start of a recession less is invested and the funds accruing are held as bank balances instead, the money stock increases as a reflection of contractionary tendencies, and this does not result in price rises.

Time and again it can be seen that exchange rates follow purchasing power parities. But it can also frequently be observed that quite a different proposition is correct: exchange rates are determined by interest rate differentials. Money flows out of a country with low interest rates and into one with high rates, and demand for the currency of the high-rate country causes that currency to appreciate. When on a market several explanations of price changes are possible, this usually leads to confusion among the market participants. How will the envisaged reduction in the public sector deficit in the United States affect dollar rates? From the standpoint of the purchasing power parity theory, the answer is: it will dampen the upward trend in prices and the dollar will appreciate. From the standpoint of the interest-rate-parity theory, the conclusion is: it will push interest rates down and the dollar will depreciate. Unless central banks offer guidance on such a market, the course of events is determined by speculation. Once speculators have set off in a given direction, they stick to it. The idea that every speculative gain is matched by a speculative loss and that, since losses of any size whatsoever cannot be borne, the swings in rates cannot become overly large, fails to appreciate that these losses often only occur in the form of lost profits. A speculator buys US dollars at DM 2.00 per dollar and sells them at DM 2.10 to another speculator who sells them in turn at DM 2.20. The first speculator may be annoyed with himself for having sold too soon, but he feels himself to be a gainer, in just the same way as the second speculator. This is how exchange rates reach levels of DM 1.71 or DM 3.47 to the dollar.

A successful national monetary policy must be based on analyses that reveal the variety of the influences operative at any one time. The growing internationalisation of world trade is increasing the number of these influences. An advantage of this process is that today it is even more obvious than before that monocausal explanations in economic analysis, and simple rules for therapy, are not adequate to cope with the complexity of the problems.

1.7   ECONOMIC POLICY STRATEGY IN AN OPEN WORLD ECONOMY

Economic policy-makers in every country have to face up to the fact that it is not only important to achieve the domestic goals of price stability, appropriate economic growth and full employment, but that a number of international problems – for example, the exchange rate problem, the debt problem and the current account problem – must be solved as well. An economic policy strategy should be so designed as to help in coming nearer to all these objectives. A strategy of this type can be described as follows: the safeguarding of non-inflationary economic growth in a monetary system largely free of disruptions.

There are two components to such a strategy. The safeguarding of non-inflationary economic growth is a task for national economic policy-makers. The emergence of a monetary system largely free of disruptions presupposes co-operation between the major countries in economic policy and on the foreign exchange markets. The European Monetary System bears witness to the fact that such co-operation is possible.

In the individual national economies, safeguarding non-inflationary growth implies strengthening potential supply and adjusting aggregate demand to this potential supply. Strengthening the potential supply means stimulating private capital formation so as to create additional jobs, thus reducing unemployment. The ideas of all economists are relevant to bringing this about; with respect to stimulating growth, those of the supply-siders are perhaps particularly useful. The aim of adjusting demand to potential supply is to achieve a nominal GNP that is moving on a path which is consistent with potential supply and on which price stability is maintained, or any residual inflation is eliminated. In this context, too, no ideas postulated in economic theory are superfluous for the implementation of economic policy – naturally not those of Keynes either. A strategy of this kind is medium term in orientation. It is designed, after all, to reach the growth rate of production potential, that is, of that GNP at which labour and plant capacities are fully utilised, while prices remain stable.

If demand can be kept on the path of potential supply, it does not 'spill over'. Price stability is maintained or inflation rates are reduced. If demand corresponds to potential supply, then the potential is fully utilised. An appropriate rate of economic growth is achieved, and this helps to cut down unemployment. If all major countries act in this way, the resultant upturn in world trade will provide the debtor countries, too, with additional scope for selling their products. Economies running a current account deficit should try to ensure that their domestic demand increases less than overall GNP. Surplus countries should do just the opposite.

National monetary policy in the individual economies will support this strategy through interest rate and liquidity policy. It will see to it that the growth rate of the monetary aggregates is consistent with the envisaged growth rate of GNP. It is always possible, particularly in an open world economy, for the monetary aggregates to deviate from the course that is consistent with envisaged nominal GNP. As long as the rise in demand is in line with the increase in potential supply, such deviations need give no cause for concern.

Economic policy strategy in an open world economy must not only safeguard non-inflationary growth in individual national economies but also make the international monetary system largely free of disruptions. 'Largely free of disruptions' means that international transactions should not be hampered by changes in exchange rates. Transactions in goods and services are not distorted, and thus disrupted, by exchange rate changes when exchange rates follow the changes in purchasing power parities ('trade neutrality'). This does not happen, as we all know, of its own accord. Hence, given the floating exchange rates for the US dollar, the yen and European currencies, it is necessary for central banks to agree to intervene. Only if such intervention is carried out jointly is it successful. It suffices if the market is told where central banks see exchange rates over the next year. Intervention points should not be set. They only constitute testing points for the market and, in the event of interventions, spark off substantial liquidity inflows and outflows. Central banks have sufficient experience of exchange market transactions to steer exchange rates where they want to have them. Once exchange rates are subject to central bank guidance, and once the market knows which way exchange rates are heading, speculation will relieve the central banks of a great deal of their work.

However, developments on the foreign exchange markets are determined not merely by transactions in goods and services, but predominantly by short and long-term capital transactions. Money and capital movements are not distorted, and thus disrupted, by exchange rate changes when exchange rates follow a trend which is in line with interest rate differentials ('capital transactions neutrality'). In this case it makes no difference whether one invests one's funds in a country with high interest rates or a land with low rates. When reconverting the foreign currency into one's own currency at the end of the period of investment, the difference is offset by the change in the exchange rate during this period.

The calls for trade neutrality and capital transactions neutrality on the foreign exchange markets can only be reconciled if central bank interventions ensure that exchange rates follow changes in purchasing power parities, and if at the same time interest rate differentials between individual countries do not deviate too much from the differences in inflation rates. Thus, keeping the international monetary system largely free of disruptions means that central banks must not only intervene, but also co-operate in their interest rate policies. In view of the importance of international short and long-term capital movements for the foreign exchange markets, such co-operation is a matter of vital significance.

It might be objected that such heavy demands on the co-operative spirit of major countries can hardly be satisfied. This may, indeed, be the case. However, it must then be recalled that there is only one alternative to co-operation: controls on capital movements and protectionism. The outlined economic policy strategy in an open world economy is designed to avoid precisely this.

Note

1. For further comments by the author on some of the issues discussed in this paper see Köhler (1988), (1990) and (1991).

References

Köhler, C. (1988) 'Economic Policy in a Framework of Internationalised Economic Relations', in P. Arestis (ed.), *Contemporary Issues in Money and Banking. Essays in Honour of Stephen Frowen* (London: Macmillan; New York: St. Martin's Press, pp. 85–101).

Köhler, C. (1990) *Internationalökonomie: Ein System offener Volkswirtschaften* (Berlin: Duncker & Humblot); English edition *The Global Economy: A System of Open Economies* (London: Edward Elgar, 1992.)

Köhler, C. (1992) 'The Unsolved Problems of the Eighties – a Challenge for the Nineties' in S. F. Frowen (ed.), *Monetary Theory and Monetary Policy: New Tracks for the 1990s* (London: Macmillan; New York: St. Martin's Press).

2 Federal Reserve Policy since October 1979: A Justified Response to Financial Innovations?

Thomas Mayer*

In recent years many financial innovations have occurred in the United States, while the Federal Reserve (Fed) has moved further away from monetarism. Are these two connected? Can the Fed's policy in recent years be interpreted as a justified response to financial innovations? I will argue that the answer is no. Some time in the future financial innovations may well make monetary targeting impossible, but so far this has not happened in the US.

2.1 THE MONETARIST(?) EXPERIMENT

Fed policy from October 1979 to around August 1982 is often referred to as a 'monetarist experiment'. Whether it deserves to be called 'monetarist' at all is a disputed matter. I will avoid this issue by referring to it as 'p-monetarist', leaving it up to the reader whether to interpret the 'p' as 'practically', 'partially' or 'pseudo'. The Fed adopted some monetarist ideas, but we live in a nonlinear world – adopting *some* monetarist ideas and not others may make policy operate less in accordance with monetarist ideas than it otherwise would. The growth rates of money, the base and reserves were *less* stable after October 1979 than before.

However, the new policy was much closer to monetarism in one important respect. It allowed interest rates to fluctuate greatly, so that maintaining interest-rate stability was no longer a serious constraint on Fed policy. Prior to October 1979 the Fed had tried to attain its monetary growth-rate targets while keeping the funds rate within a narrow band. When these two objectives clashed the Federal

Open Market Committee (FOMC) gave preference to its fund rate target, and hence lost control over the monetary growth rate. The main reason why the Fed lost control over the money supply and generated high inflation was not that the FOMC was targeting interest rates instead of an aggregate, but rather that it was not adjusting its interest rate target to the necessary extent. Had the FOMC been willing to allow sharp swings in the funds rate whenever shifts in the IS curve[1] generated changes in the demand for money, it might perhaps have been able to stabilise nominal gross national product (GNP) as effectively with an interest rate target as with a money-growth target. But like so many government agencies, the Fed tried to stabilise a price, the interest rate, and then was unhappy about losing control over the quantity. The Fed's experience prior to October 1979 does not tell us that the funds rate is an inferior instrument to, say, total reserves *in the world usually assumed in economic models*; that is a world in which the central bank acts rationally and is not subject to overwhelming political pressures. It does tell us that, given the political realities in the United States, the Fed cannot control the monetary growth rate if it is perceived as setting interest rates.

To break the expectations of accelerating inflation that were threatening the financial system the Fed had to get out of the business of explicitly and openly controlling interest rates. In this respect the p-monetarist experiment was highly successful. It gave the Fed the freedom to undertake the painful policies that were needed.

But in another way it was a dismal failure. The Fed paid the price of allowing much greater fluctuations in interest rates, but it did not get the reward of a stable monetary growth rate. The variance of the federal funds rate rose greatly – but so did the variance of the money growth rate.[2] The increase in the variability of the funds rate was not quite as large as it seems at first glance for two reasons. First, since interest rates were much higher after October 1979 than before, the change is less dramatic when expressed as a percentage of the mean interest rate rather than as a given number of percentage points. Second, in the decade and a half just prior to the p-monetarist experiment, interest rates had been unusually stable by historical standards. As Harvey Rosenblum and Steven Storin (1983, p. 13) have pointed out, if measured by the *percentage* change of the funds rate, then, in the context of the entire period since 1953, the volatility of the funds rate in the early 1980s, was 'neither unknown [in the past] nor excessive'. And the percentage change in the interest rate is a better measure of its macroeconomic impact than is the absolute change (see Rasche, 1985).

As discussed in detail elsewhere (Mayer, 1989) the increased variance of the monetary growth rate should not be attributed in a simple way, either to the Fed's flawed operating procedures, such as the use of lagged reserve requirement, as is done by monetarists, or to an inherent impossibility of controlling the monetary growth rate, as many Keynesians believe. Instead, it was due to a number of factors. The growth rates of the base and reserves did become more variable but, at least in an arithmetic decomposition, a much greater part of the increase in the variance of the M1 growth rate was due to an increased variance of the money multiplier. Moreover, changes in the covariance of the base and its multiplier also contributed to the increased monthly variance of M1. Much of the increased variance of the multiplier, in turn, resulted from a rise in the variance of the currency ratio, a rise that is hard to explain, and *may* have been coincidental to the p-monetarist experiment.

2.2   THE END OF THE MONETARIST(?) EXPERIMENT

Around late summer or early fall of 1982 the Fed changed both its policy and policy procedures. It declared an armistice in the war against inflation, so that it could fight two other enemies, recession and the danger of a national and international financial collapse. To do so it adopted an operating procedure that was more accommodative of changes in the demand for money and is, in fact, similar to the operating procedure it used prior to October 1979 (see Rasche, 1985).

This new operating procedure results in interest-rate stability because it amounts to accommodating almost fully short-run shifts in the demand for money, whether caused by movements of IS or LM. The Fed now targets borrowed reserves rather than unborrowed reserves. Hence, if the demand for money rises and banks borrow more, the Fed provides sufficient unborrowed reserves through open-market operations to bring borrowed reserves back to their target level, thus accommodating the demand for reserves and money. What makes a borrowed reserves target much more accommodative than an unborrowed reserves target is that if the Fed targets borrowed reserves, then a rise in the demand for money, and hence in the demand for borrowed reserves, does not generate a higher funds rate, but results in the Fed providing additional unborrowed reserves at an unchanged funds rate. With the Fed providing enough unborrowed reserves to balance any increase in the demand for reserves, the funds rate need not rise when the demand for money increases.[3] By contrast, under the previous operating procedure banks were driven to increase their borrowings from the Fed when the demand for money rose. Being reluctant to borrow from the Fed they drove up the funds rate.

In setting its original target for borrowings the Fed selects that borrowing level that it thinks will generate the funds rate it desires. Hence the Fed controls the funds rate indirectly. Except to the extent that it makes errors in estimating the function relating borrowing to the funds rate, such an indirect control works the same way as the direct control over the funds rate that the Fed exercised prior to October 1979. Not surprisingly, the funds rate has been stable. From October 1982 to December 1986 the mean absolute variation in the monthly mean of the 90-day Treasury bill rate was 0.26 per cent, compared to 28 per cent for October 1975 to September 1979. Expressed as percentages of the mean bill rates these figures become 3.3 per cent for October 1982 to December 1986, and 4.4 per cent for October 1975 to September 1979.

Although the new procedure is almost the same as the one prior to October 1979, it does have a great political advantage. It hides the fact that the Fed controls interest rates, something that will become useful sooner or later when the Fed will want to reduce the growth rate of money and let interest rates rise.

What has happened to monetary targets in all this? They have obviously been downgraded. Indeed, one may question whether the Fed really has monetary targets at all. To be sure, the Federal Open Market Committee (FOMC) announces certain monetary targets, but what does it mean by 'targets'? The relevant definition of a 'target' given in Webster's *Dictionary* is: 'a goal set or proposed for achievement'. This meaning is consistent with the FOMC's frequent reference to a certain monetary growth rate as 'acceptable', which implies that other monetary growth rates are not acceptable.

However, in the 1985 *Annual Report* of the Federal Reserve Bank of Minneapolis, its president, Gary Stern, described the Fed's monetary 'targeting' in a quite different way, a way that shows it not to be targeting at all, at least in the dictionary sense of the term.[3] In his view, instead of being a goal that the Fed tries to reach:

what the money ranges are meant to be are indicators to the public of the general course of monetary policy *if the economy performs as expected* . . . Any specific ranges tell the public just what the Fed's actions will imply for the growth of money during that period if the usual economic patterns persist . . . *In this strategy the Fed's money measures are not targeted.* They are, instead among the many variables the Fed uses to determine how next to aim at its goals by adjusting its instruments. The money targets are thus known as *information variables.* . . . Unlike targeting, the information variable strategy uses all available information . . . If an information variable were targeted, the Fed's efforts to keep it on target might make the Fed ignore information that other variables were offering about its real goals . . . This best way to conduct monetary policy is quite different from the view that many people seem to have of the Fed's strategy . . . The Fed does not in a strict sense target these measures. (Stern, 1986, pp. 3–5, first two italics added.)

Stern's description of targets is not clear. In most of the cited passage the money ranges are described essentially as forecasts of a variable that is merely a by-product of the policy, and the actual money-growth rate as just one of several variables the Fed considers in deciding on policy. Neither of these two meanings corresponds to what is generally meant by a 'target'. Then in the last sentence we are told that these are not targets 'in a strict sense'. This is perfectly correct, but then, according to Stern's previous statements neither are they targets in a loose sense.

If Stern is describing the Fed's 'monetary targeting' correctly, then it is doubtful that money should be called a 'target' at all. But, at least now, if not at the time that Stern was writing, M2 does seem to function as a genuine target variable. I don't mean with this that the FOMC adopts that policy that it thinks will cause M2 to reach its target, but only that the M2 growth rate is *one* of the targets the Fed aims at. Excessive growth in M2 is likely to cause the FOMC to moderate its expansionary policy, at least to some extent. The experience of the 1970s has not been entirely forgotten. Moreover, the FOMC is afraid that excessive monetary growth would cause financial markets to expect higher inflation, and hence to raise interest rates. Thirdly, the Fed can use an excessive monetary growth rate as a justification for an unpopular restrictive policy.

The Fed's method of controlling the money stock, that is setting the funds rate at the level that will induce the public to demand the right amount of money, is not feasible if the interest elasticity of money demand is too low. With a low enough interest elasticity tight control over the monetary growth rate might require greater interest rate variability than the Fed is willing to tolerate.[4]

Two financial innovations, the demise of Regulation Q, that set ceilings on the interest rate paid on time deposits and the spread of interest bearing checkable deposits, could *in principle* reduce substantially the interest elasticity of the demand for money. But while this might become a problem in the future, so far interest payments on money, and the end of Regulation Q ceilings, have not lowered the interest elasticity of the demand for money. According to Wenninger (1986) the interest elasticity of M1 has, if anything, risen, though with only a few years' data available the evidence for a rise can hardly be called strong. David Lindsey (in Darby, *et al.*, 1987) also found that financial deregulation and advances in cash management have raised the interest elasticity of M1. The elasticity may well have risen because the rates paid on times deposits move flexibly with market rates, while the rates paid on 'other checkable deposits', such as NOW (negotiable order of withdrawal) accounts, that are included in M1 move sluggishly. If time deposits and NOW accounts are closer substitutes than are time deposits and demand deposits, then one would expect the introduction of 'other checkable deposits' to increase the interest elasticity of M1.

But even if a financial innovation, such as the demise of Regulation Q, does not lower the interest elasticity of the demand for money, it could still make it harder to control the growth rate of money by increasing the standard error of the money-demand equation that the Fed used in controlling the growth rate of money. But it does not seem plausible that concern about the impact of financial innovations on the efficacy of its operating procedures played much of a direct role in the Fed's switch away from meaningful monetary targeting.

What was surely much more important in the Fed's shift away from monetary targeting is that M1 velocity, instead of growing at a stable 3.2 per cent annual rate as before, now became more erratic, and fell. In the period 1981–1986 M1 velocity has fallen by 16 per cent. Since in the early 1980s the Fed had set its monetary targets on the assumption that velocity would continue to grow, monetary policy became much too tight. The US experienced its worst recession since the 1930s. There were fears of a massive financial collapse, both at home and in the less developed countries (LDCs), and Congress threatened the Fed with dire retribution.

This is not to deny that – apart from the indirect effects through changes in velocity – financial innovations played *some* role in the demise of monetary targeting. The Fed *was* concerned about what the rise of various interest-paying transactions accounts was doing to the meaning of M1, and at times, such as at the expiration of the 'All Savers' accounts, had to make allowances for special disturbances to M1. But the collapse of M1 velocity was surely a more important factor.

Hence, if one wants to attribute the demise of monetary targeting to financial innovations one must argue that these innovations were responsible for unpredictable changes in the trend of velocity or for velocity being less stable relative to its trend. Is this plausible? The decline in the trend of velocity was surely, in large part, due to the drop in the cost of holding money as interest rates fell along with the inflation rate. Financial innovations did, however, play some part too. As David Lindsey points out, they increased the interest elasticity of M1 (Darby *et al.*, 1987), so that velocity fell by more, as interest rates declined, than it would have done in the absence of financial innovations.

Whether innovations were also responsible for shifts in the demand for money in a more direct way is controversial. On the one hand, Stephen Miller (1986) suggests that financial innovations are responsible for substantial prediction errors in the money demand function. He attributes the downward adjustment of the demand for money that started in 1973 to a decline in the competitive position of banks as Regulation Q raised the opportunity cost of holding deposits. Then, when Regulation Q was phased out, the public responded by again holding more deposits, so that velocity fell.[5] On the other hand, John Judd and Bharat Trehan (1987, p. 2) argue that the direct effect of financial innovations cannot account for the fall in velocity. They point out that 'the bulk of the evidence suggests that before 1985, the velocity of M1 did not undergo sustained downward shifts related to deregulation, despite several episodes of major deregulation in the early 1980s'.

Apart from the trend of velocity, has innovation also substantially raised the variance of velocity relative to its trend or made the demand function for money much more unstable? Given the small number of data-points available so far, I doubt that one will be able to answer this question for several years still.

2.3 SHOULD THE FED HAVE ABANDONED M1 TARGETING?

To say that financial innovations were a cause of the shift away from M1 targeting is not the same as saying that they *justified* this shift to another target. It is easy to show that M1 is not an ideal target, but other targets may be even worse. I will first discuss a change to interest rate and GNP targets, and then to M2 and M3 targets.

But first note that despite financial innovations, monetary targeting is still appropriate as long as the monetary target is set in a way that takes account of velocity changes. However, it is not clear that this can be done simply by assuming that this period's velocity will be equal to last period's velocity (see Mayer, 1987, 1988; Meltzer, 1987; Modigliani, 1988). Monetary targeting is not the same as a monetary rule. It does not require the Fed to stay with a specific monetary growth rate into the indefinite future when there occur substantial unanticipated changes in the trend of velocity. Admittedly, the great instability of velocity in the 1980s has weakened the case for M1 targeting. But it has not destroyed this case because the desirability of a policy must be judged against the desirability of the alternative policies.

A traditional alternative to M1 targeting has been interest-rate targeting. Would that have been good policy? Surely not, because the relation between the interest rate and GNP has also changed. The US experienced an unusually long, though admittedly slow expansion, accompanied by extraordinarily high real interest rates. Suppose the Fed had stuck with targeting interest rates. To make a favourable case for interest-rate targeting assume that the Fed, having been convinced by the experience of the 1970s that the nominal rate is a bad target, had picked as its target a real rate. In an attempt to lower the real rate to the level that has traditionally been consistent with an expansion, it would have raised the money-growth rate by much more than it actually did. The result would probably have been an increase in the inflation rate substantial enough to force the Fed to abandon its interest-rate target. Several recent studies of the effect of an increase in the monetary growth rate on interest rates found that there no longer is a meaningful liquidity effect from a higher growth rate of money (see Reichenstein, 1987). If these studies are correct – and not all the evidence support them – then even a highly inflationary rise in the money-growth rate may do relatively little to lower the real rate.[6] The real rate would then fall only to the extent that the Fisher effect is not fully operative.

Hence, despite the recent instability of M1 velocity, an interest-rate target may be worse than a money-growth target. This is so particularly because political pressures would make it much harder for the Fed to abandon a low interest-rate target than a money-growth target when either target turns out to be too expansionary.

How about a nominal GNP target? With a GNP target, as with a money-growth target, the central bank first selects its desired level of nominal GNP. It then estimates actual GNP in the absence of a change in monetary policy, and modifies its monetary policy enough to bring its new estimate of GNP to the desired level. Can the Fed estimate GNP accurately enough for this? This is hard to say. In the 1980s GNP forecasts have been much less accurate than in the 1970s. Stephen McNees (1985, p. 37) shows the accuracy of forecasts of a sample of forecasters for 1971.2–1985.1. For the period prior to 1980 the mean absolute error was 1.6 per cent, but for 1980.1–1985.1 it was 2.9 per cent, almost twice as large. Victor Zarnowitz (1986, p. 7) has explained the decline in the accuracy of nominal GNP forecasts by the greater frequency and severity of recessions in this period and by the unexpectedly severe disinflation.

Hence, if the use of a GNP target instead of a monetary target would have caused the 1980s to be no more depressed than the 1970s, a nominal GNP target should have worked equally well in both periods. But since the inflation rate had to be brought down, the period since 1980 would have been afflicted with worse recessions than the 1970s, regardless of which target the Fed used. And with more severe recessions a GNP target would have been less effective in the early 1980s than it would have been in the 1970s.

But the real question is not whether a GNP target would have worked as well in the 1980s as in the 1970s, but whether a GNP target would have led to a better policy than the policy actually followed by the Fed, with its partial reliance on M1 targets. This too is hard to determine, in part because the distinction between a nominal GNP target and a monetary target is a subtle one. A central bank that uses monetary targets surely selects a particular growth rate of money because of the level of GNP that this monetary growth rate implies, so that it does have a GNP target at one remove. Similarly, if a central bank uses a GNP target it must also use a monetary or base measure, or else an interest rate, as an intermediate target since it can aim at GNP almost only via these variables. The essential difference between a GNP target and a monetary target is that if the central bank announces a monetary target it is less likely to change the monetary growth rate as new information comes in, because to do so means to lose credibility. By contrast, if it announces a GNP target it can change the growth rate of money at no cost to itself.

Given the uncertainties about the behaviour of velocity, one can make an argument that if ever there was a time for targeting nominal GNP other than money, the period since 1980 was it. By hindsight, at least, it is clear that in 1982 the Fed should have abandoned its monetary growth targets earlier than it did.

However, one can also make the opposite argument. The Fed is not an independent agent removed from political pressures. These pressures push it in the direction of excessive expansion. Hence, at a time when a substantial disinflation is needed the Fed requires some protection from political pressures. Tying itself to the mast by announcing M1 targets gives it some needed protection.

Thus, despite the recent behaviour of M1 velocity, interest rates or nominal GNP would not *necessarily* have been preferable targets.

2.4 TARGETING M2 OR M3

Even if one concludes that M1 should not be targeted, monetary targeting is still feasible by targeting M2 or M3, which add to M1 certain non-transaction components, mainly small savings and time deposits for M2, and all savings and time deposits for M3. These two measures internalise much of the shift between M1 and other assets, and they are thus much less affected by financial innovations. (See Judd and Trehan, 1987.) Although the growth-trends of both M2 velocity and M3 velocity did fall in the 1980s relative to the 1970s, they declined much less than did the trend of M1 velocity. Moreover, the demand functions for M2 and M3 do not show instability. The errors of their out-of-sample forecasts for 1985 and 1986 are not out of line with their within-sample standard errors (Judd and Trehan, 1987). In a remarkable paper Jeffrey Hallman, Richard Porter and

David Small (1989) have shown that the velocity of M2 has been stable enough to allow one to predict the price level from a knowledge of M2.

So why not target M2 or M3? Two objections can be raised. First, a switch to M2 or M3 is just ad hocery, and there is no reason to expect M2 or M3 velocity to be stable in the future. By itself the accusation of ad hocery, while correct, is not so serious. Ad hocery, and other defensive manoeuvres, are mortal sins in constructing a theory, but we are concerned here, not with a theory, but with a policy-guide. For example, suppose that the data were to show that for some unknown reason velocity each quarter is equal to 103 per cent of velocity six quarters earlier. This would hardly be an acceptable theory. But if this relation persists, it would be an extremely useful guide for monetary policy.

But while the ad hocery charge therefore does not *absolutely* prohibit a shift to M2 or M3 targeting, it should by no means be dismissed entirely. We have a well-developed theory, the quantity theory, that explains a stable relation between the supply of the medium of exchange or other extremely liquid assets and GNP, but it is at least somewhat harder to explain a stable relation between the sum of all the components in M2 or M3 and GNP. Hence, there is a danger that the stability we observe is not causal, and thus will not persist when we try to manipulate GNP by manipulating M2. On the other hand, the velocity of M2 has been stable for the period over which M1 velocity was stable, and also stable during the 1980s when M1 velocity was unstable. Hence, I am willing to advocate a switch to M2 or M3 targeting, and with some trepidation take the risk that Goodhart's law will strike again.

The second problem with using M2 or M3 is that the Fed cannot control it in the way recommended by monetarists, that is by controlling the base or reserves. Personal time deposits have no reserve requirement, and nonpersonal time deposits have a much smaller reserve requirement than do checkable deposits. Hence banks can increase M2 and M3 relatively easily by inducing some depositors to switch out of checkable deposits into time or savings deposits. The Fed therefore has to control M2 and M3 from the demand side by setting the funds rate so that the public will want to hold the appropriate amount of M2 or M3. But this is no different from what the Fed has been doing all along in controlling M1.

If the Fed therefore has to set an interest rate, even when it is using a monetary target, what difference does it then make whether the

Fed has an M2 target or not? The difference is that with an interest-rate target the Fed has to select that funds rate that it considers appropriate for its GNP target, while with an M2 target it selects that funds rate that it thinks will generate the appropriate level of M2, and it then relies on a predictable relation between M2 and GNP. If the combined error terms in predicting the funds rate-M2 relation and the M2-GNP relation are smaller than the single error term in predicting the funds rate-GNP relation, then the M2 target is obviously useful. This may well be the case because the funds rate-GNP relation is a complex one that involves a poorly understood term-structure equation. Moreover, since the funds rate-M2 relation has a shorter lag than the funds rate-GNP relation, the former allows the Fed less of an excuse to procrastinate in changing the funds rate. Furthermore, explicitly targeting money rather than interest rates reduces the political pressure to be too expansionary. Along the same lines, since money is clearly a stock, focusing on money probably induces the Fed to pay more attention to the long-run effects of its policies, than a focus on interest rates would. Much of the case for a monetary target is political rather than a matter of optimal control theory.

2.5 FINANCIAL INNOVATIONS AND M1 TARGETING IN THE FUTURE

One can tell two seemingly plausible – but contradictory – stories about what will happen in the future. One is that the rate at which financial innovations occurred in the US during the 1970s and early 1980s was unusual, and will not be sustained. According to this story, the rapid pace of financial innovations was the result of three factors, the spread of the computer revolution, a high inflation rate that generated a great rise in nominal interest rates, and Regulation Q ceilings that fostered the development of financial instruments and practices to avoid these ceilings. It is not likely that the costs of electronic transfers will continue to fall at such a rapid pace as before, nominal interest rates will probably not rise very sharply, and Regulation Q is finally gone. Hence, financial innovations are likely to be fewer, and velocity will become more predictable again.

The other story is that M1 velocity is inherently unstable, that the stable trend of M1 velocity from the mid-1950s to the end of the 1970s, was an aberration. Thus in the prior period, 1890–1929, trend-adjusted velocity was not very stable (see Mayer, 1987). According to this story the success of the postwar revival of the quantity theory can in large part be explained as a futile attempt to generalise from a particular and atypical behaviour of velocity. (However, as Friedman has pointed out, an inability to predict velocity hardly enhances the case for discretionary policy). Incidentally, the fact that after adjusting for trend, M1 velocity was stable in the 1960s and 1970s does not increase one's faith in the argument that financial innovations must surely make velocity unstable. The 1960s and 1970s saw a great financial innovation; the rise of thrift deposits relative to commercial bank deposits. In December 1959 deposits in nonbank thrift institutions equalled 65 per cent of old M1. In December 1979 they equalled 176 per cent. Gurley and Shaw's *Money in a Theory of Finance*, the fountainhead of the argument that financial innovations have dethroned money and its consort, velocity, was published in 1960, and despite the cogent case that it made, velocity had a stable trend for the next nineteen years.

Will velocity be predictable if M1 includes interest-paying transactions accounts that are repositories for savings? Many economists think that such a development makes velocity harder to predict because the demand for money then depends upon the whole spectrum of interest rates on assets that compete for the public's savings. Moreover, Bharat Trehan and Carl Walsh (1987) have argued that if transactions accounts and time deposits become close substitutes, then their relative quantities will become more dependent on conditions of supply, that is on the types of deposits that banks want to issue. Moreover, the data do suggest that in 1985 and 1986, the inclusion of savings components did make M1 velocity less stable (see Judd and Trehan, 1987). But then a simple solution would be to switch to an M2 or M3 target.

Furthermore, even if, as happened in the 1960s, financial innovations do not cause M1 velocity to become unstable, they could make M1 targeting much more difficult by reducing the interest-elasticity of the demand for M1, so that controlling M1 would require much greater fluctuations in interest rates. While, as previously discussed, this has not happened so far, it might occur in the future; depository institutions might start to adjust the yield on transactions accounts much more flexibly to market yields than they do now. But it is far from certain that they will do so. To be fully effective increases in deposit rates have to be advertised extensively, and this makes it costly to change them frequently. And again, any resulting problem would be less severe for M2 and M3 targeting than for M1 targeting. Moreover, in a world with as well-developed interest-rate hedges as we have now, the economic damage done by sharp fluctuations in interest rates should not be so great. However, given the rise in the number of variable interest-rate mortgages outstanding, the political damage to the Fed may be great.

2.6 CONCLUSION

One theme that does emerge loud and clear from this rather diffuse contest of 'on the one hand' vs 'but on the other hand' is that financial innovations have greatly strengthened the case for targeting M2 or M3 rather than M1. The Fed's abandonment of M1 targeting may well be justified.

But financial innovations have generated much less of a case for abandoning monetary targeting altogether. The advantages that an M1 target has over targeting interest rates or GNP are essentially shared by M2 and M3 targets, and these targets are much less vulnerable to financial innovations that destabilise velocity. Hence, it may well be that the main impact of financial innovations on monetary targeting will be to change the type of monetary targets used, and not to cause monetary targeting to be abandoned. I must, however, add a qualification: It is certainly possible that in the future financial innovations will make M2 and M3 targeting inefficient by causing M2 and M3 velocities to become erratic.

The future of monetary targeting will also depend on the behaviour of the inflation rate. If the inflation rate rises the Fed may decide to pay more attention again to monetary targets, because monetary targeting provides it with more freedom to fight inflation. A major benefit of monetary targeting is that it allows the Fed to say to those who complain about high and rising interest rates: 'So sorry, we just control reserves and money, and we are not responsible for interest rates.' It is hard to predict how seriously the Fed will actually have to take its monetary targets for such an argument to be credible.

To be sure, in the *very* long run, when the computer revolution has greatly increased the liquidity of many assets, and world capital markets have become much more integrated, the distinction between domestic money and other domestic and foreign assets will eventually shrink enough to make monetary targeting infeasible (see Pierce, 1986). But that brave new world is still some distance away.

Notes

*I am indebted for helpful comments to Thomas Cargill, Milton Friedman, Kevin Hoover and Raymond Lombra.

1. For a discussion of the IS–LM curves see Gordon (1991, Ch. 5).
2. For data on the variability of interest rates see Rasche (1985).
3. An economist at the Richmond Federal Reserve Bank, Robert Hetzel (1986), explained the Fed's use of monetary targets along the same lines as Stern.
4. This is so, not only under the Fed's current operating procedure, but would be true also with a total reserves or base procedure.
5. For an excellent discussion of the impact of financial innovations prior to 1980 see Judd, Trehan and Scadding (1982).
6. The Fed's econometric model shows a liquidity effect of money on interest rates (see Brayton and Mauskopf, 1987).

References

Brayton, F. and Mauskopf, E. (1987) 'Structure and Use of the MPS Quarterly Econometric Model of the United States', *Federal Reserve Bulletin*, 73, February, pp. 93–109.

Darby, M., Poole, W., Lindsey, D., Friedman, M. and Bazdarich, M. (1987) 'Recent Behavior of the Velocity of Money', *Contemporary Policy Issues*, 5, January, pp. 1–32.

Gordon, R. J. (1991) *Macroeconomics*, 5th edn, Seranton, Penn., Harper & Row.

Gurley, R. and Shaw, E., (1960), *Money in a Theory of Finance* (Washington, DC.: Brookings Institution).

Hallman, J., Porter, R. and Small, D. (1989) *M2 per Unit of Potential GNP as an Anchor for the Price Level*, Washington, DC, Board of Governors, Federal Reserve System, Staff Study, No. 157.

Hetzel, R. (1986) 'A Congressional Mandate for Monetary Policy', *Cato Journal*, 5, Winter, pp. 797–820.

Judd, J. and Trehan, B. (1987) 'Downgrading M-1', Federal Reserve Bank of San Francisco, *Weekly Letter*, 13 March.

Judd, J., Trehan, B. and Scadding, J. (1982) 'The Search for a Stable Money Demand Function', *Journal of Economic Literature*, 20, September, pp. 993–1023.

Lodsey, David (1983) 'Nonborrowed Reserves Targeting and Monetary Control,' in Laurence Meyer (ed.) *Improving Money Stock Control*, Boston, Kluwer-Nijhoff, pp. 3–40.

Lodsey, David *et al.* (1984) 'Short-Run Monetary Control: Evidence under a Non-Borrowed Reserves Operating Procedure,' *Journal of Monetary Economics*, 13, January, pp. 87–111.

Lombra, Michael (1980) 'Monetary Control: Consensus or Confusion?',

Federal Reserve Bank of Boston, *Controlling Monetary Aggregates III* Boston, Federal Reserve Bank of Boston.

Mayer, T. (1987) 'Replacing the FOMC by a PC', *Contemporary Policy Issues*, 5.

Mayer, T. (1988) 'Modigliani on Monetarism: A Response', *Contemporary Policy Issues*, 6, October, 19–24.

Mayer, T. (1989) 'The Instability of M-1 during the Claimed Monetarist Experiment', Working Paper, University of California, Davis, pp. 570–97.

Mayer, T. (1992) 'Monetarism in a World Without "Money"', in S. F. Frowen (ed.) *Monetary Theory and Monetary Policy: New Tracks for the 1990s* (London: Macmillan; New York: St. Martin's Press).

McNees, S. (1985) 'Which Forecast Should You Use?', Federal Bank of Boston, *New England Economic Review*, July/August, pp. 36–42.

Meltzer, A. (1987) 'Limits of Short-Run Stabilization Policy', *Economic Inquiry*, 25, January, pp. 1–14.

Miller, S. (1986) 'Financial Innovation, Depository-Institution Deregulation and the Demand for Money', *Journal of Macroeconomics*, 8, Summer, pp. 279–96.

Modigliani, F. (1988) 'The Monetarist Controversy Revisited', *Contemporary Policy Issues*, 6, October, pp. 3–18.

Pierce, J. (1986) 'Financial Reform in the United States and the Financial System of the Future', in Yoshio Suzuki and Hiroshi Yomo (eds) *Financial Innovation and Monetary Policy: Asia and the West* (Tokyo: University of Tokyo Press, pp. 183–202).

Rasche, R. (1985) 'Interest Rate Volatility and Alternative Monetary Control Procedures', Federal Reserve Bank of San Francisco, *Economic Review*, Summer, pp. 46–63.

Reichenstein, W. (1987) 'The Impact of Money on Short-Term Interest Rates', *Economic Inquiry*, 25, January, pp. 67–82.

Rosenblum, H. and Storin, S. (1983) 'Interest Rate Volatility in Historical Perspective', Federal Reserve Bank of Chicago, *Economic Perspectives*, 7, January/February, pp. 10–19.

Stern, G. (1986) 'The Fed's Money Supply Ranges: Still Useful After All These Years', in Federal Reserve Bank of Minneapolis, *1985 Annual Report*, Minneapolis, Min., pp. 1–15.

Trehan, B. and Walsh, C. (1987) 'Portfolio Substitution and Recent M-1 Behavior', *Contemporary Policy Issues*, 5, January, pp. 54–63.

Wenninger, J. (1986) 'Responsiveness of Interest Rate Spreads and Deposit Flows to Changes in Market Rates', Federal Reserve Bank of New York, *Quarterly Review*, 11, Autumn, pp. 1–21.

Zarnowitz, V. (1986) 'The Record and Improvability of Economic Forecasting', National Bureau of Economic Research, Working Paper No. 2099.

3 The Control of Monetary Aggregates in the Federal Republic of Germany under Changing Conditions

Norbert Kloten

3.1 THE STRATEGY OF MONETARY TARGETING

The quality of a monetary policy can be gauged by the extent to which it succeeds in fulfilling the functions allocated to it. The Bundesbank Act assigns the Deutsche Bundesbank the task of 'safeguarding the currency'. There has been little dispute in West Germany to date that this means primarily that monetary-policy action must be geared to the goal of domestic price level stability. If the price trend in West Germany is considered on a long-term basis, it becomes clear that the Bundesbank has generally come fairly close to this goal, even though it was unable to completely prevent price development in West Germany from following the international inflation trend during phases of world-wide inflation.

The Bundesbank's successful monetary policy – successful not least by comparison with other countries – is linked to a very large extent to the strategy of monetary targeting, a course which the Bundesbank was the first central bank to adopt. It first saw the light of day in March 1973, when the Bretton Woods system finally collapsed. The transition to flexible exchange rates created the basic prerequisite for systematic control of the money stock. The elimination of the intervention obligation *vis-à-vis* the dollar meant that the central bank could no longer be forced by external influences to make available more central bank money than was appropriate from the stability viewpoint. The Bundesbank made immediate use of this scope for independent money stock control. It discarded its previous monetary indicator, the 'free liquid reserves', replacing it with the 'central bank money stock'. In order to exercise as direct a form of control as possible over the creation of central bank money, it reduced the formerly generous free liquid reserves, which allowed the banks access to central bank money at all times, to 'practically zero'.

This change of strategy was in line with the economic conceptions prevailing at the time. In view of the accelerating world-wide inflation and employment problems which were at most of a minor nature, the Keynesian paradigm was being increasingly replaced by monetarist viewpoints. In West Germany the Council of Economic Experts had already advocated a money stock-oriented course in its 1972 annual report,[1] and the economists who sympathised with monetarist views had long been criticising the use of the 'free liquid reserves' as an indicator.

To start with, the Bundesbank refrained from publicly announcing specific targets for the central bank money stock. However, once the consequences of the first oil price dictate (OPEC I) had led, in 1974, to exceptionally high wage agreements which were in conflict with the central bank's stability-oriented intentions and monetary-policy action, a target for the central bank money stock was announced for the first time in December 1974. This practice has continued up to the present day and has since been adopted by numerous other central banks.

3.2 THE DERIVATION OF MONETARY TARGETS

Precise determination is essential if a strategy of monetary targeting is to be transformed into a central bank's actual monetary policy.

The key feature of monetary control is the definition of an indicator and intermediate target to which monetary policy must be geared. The Bundesbank opted for the construct of the 'central bank money stock'. This is defined as the total of currency in circulation in the hands of non-banks and

- sight deposits multiplied by a factor of 0.166,
- time deposits for less than four years multiplied by a factor of 0.124, and
- savings deposits multiplied by a factor of 0.081.

These factors correspond to the average reserve ratios in January 1974. The central bank money stock thus consists of the currency in circulation and the required minimum reserves at constant reserve ratios on the basis of January 1974.

This definition shows that the central bank money stock has a very close affinity with the money stock M3, as both aggregates incorporate the same assets, merely weighting them differently. In the past, the central bank money stock and M3 developed largely in parallel (see Figure 3.1). Despite its designation, therefore, the central bank money stock as defined by the Bundesbank cannot be classified under the heading of the monetarist 'monetary base concepts'. This is already demonstrated by the fact that the central bank money stock includes neither excess reserves nor minimum reserves on foreign liabilities, both of which can in principle serve as a basis for domestic monetary expansion. These two elements – which are fairly insignificant in quantitative terms – are logically included in the construct of the 'adjusted central bank money stock' which the Council of Economic Experts chose as an indicator of monetary stimuli. However, this reflects above all a difference of opinion as regards the function of such a money stock aggregate. Whereas from the more monetarist viewpoint the monetary base is to be regarded primarily as an indicator of a central bank's money supply, the central bank money stock – as seen by the Bundesbank – is an intermediate target variable intended to reflect monetary expansion within the banking sector which has already taken place. This, however, clearly also reveals diverging views regarding the technique of monetary control.

Given the orientation towards the demand side of the money creation process, it would have been possible for the Bundesbank to use a money stock aggregate such as the money stock M1, M2 or M3, instead of the central bank money stock. Econometric studies have demonstrated for certain time periods fairly stable money demand functions, regardless of the definition of the money stock (except M2), so that all the other aggregates could likewise have been used as monetary targets.[2] However, the development of the money stock M1 is influenced to a very large extent by changes in short-term interest rates, so that control of this aggregate from year to year would have required reliable interest forecasts and substantially varying targets over the course of time, something which would scarcely have been compatible with the goal of stabilising expectations as regards the monetary framework. By comparison with the money stock M3, the central bank money stock has the advantage that the data are available roughly two weeks earlier and, what is more, relate to the monthly average rather than to end-of-month figures. On account of the high proportion of cash it contains, however, random shocks in the demand for cash can lead for a short

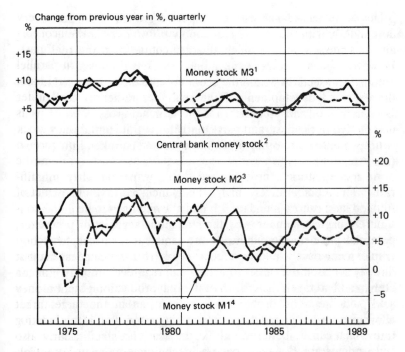

Change from previous year in %, quarterly

Figure 3.1 West German money stock and central bank money stock, 1975–89

Notes: 1. M3 = currency, sight deposits, time deposits for less than 4 years, savings deposits at *statutory notice*.

2. Central bank money stock = currency in circulation plus required minimum reserves on domestic deposits (at constant reserve ratios, base: January 1974).

3. M2 = M3 excluding savings deposits at statutory notice.

4. M1 = currency and sight deposits.

time to the inadequate impression of a far too excessive monetary expansion, although such developments have in the past always quickly returned to normal. The decision to use the central bank money stock as an intermediate target variable does not mean, of course, that the other monetary aggregates are totally disregarded in monetary analysis and thus also in the Bundesbank's monetary-policy action.

The characteristic feature of the Bundesbank's concept is a medium-term orientation designed to place monetary policy on a stable footing. This is achieved by endeavouring to ensure that the forecast rate of growth for the central bank money stock is, in principle, in accordance with the expected growth of the production potential, which reflects the real supply *possibilities* in the economy and therefore follows a much steadier course than the real GNP. However, as the central bank money stock is supposed to finance nominal transactions within the economy, the target is geared, not to the expected development of the real, but rather to that of the *nominal production potential* (not the nominal gross national product, GNP). In the past, and particularly during the initial years of the concept's existence, other factors also had to be taken into account (see Appendix 3.1).

As money stock control started during a period when inflation rates were comparatively high, the Bundesbank would not have fulfilled its statutory mandate if it had allowed itself to be guided – in a purely passive manner – by the status quo forecast of production potential price development. At the same time, unacceptably high employment risks would have been involved if the Bundesbank had directly set itself the target of achieving price-level stability immediately, and had taken the growth of the real production potential as its sole guideline. The problem was solved in that the target made allowance for an *'unavoidable increase in prices'*, that is, an inflation rate which can be bettered only at the cost of a stabilisation crisis. With price stability having been achieved once more in West Germany in the course of 1984, the target is now based directly – as already described – on the growth of the nominal production potential. During the first few years of monetary targeting, provision was also made for an *allowance for the expected additional utilisation* of the production potential. This was necessary because the strategy of monetary targeting was launched, not in a year of economic equilibrium, but instead during a recession. Seen in purely mechanistic terms, therefore, the increase in the central bank money stock was bound to exceed the growth of the production potential until the economy regained the equilibrium of full employment; otherwise monetary policy would have carried forward the recession level as the basis for future development of the production potential. Once 'equilibrium' had been achieved in 1979, changes in the utilisation of the production potential were no longer taken into account in derivation of the targets, as this would have been contrary to the medium-term orientation of monetary policy. From this time on it was possible to assume that the money supply had achieved a balanced basis, for example, a point from which increasing utilisation of the production potential is accompanied by a corresponding cyclically induced increase in the 'velocity of circulation' of the central bank money stock – and vice versa. At the same time it thereby becomes clear that short-term changes in the velocity of circulation in principle have no relevance for the targets. It is more difficult to make allowance in the money stock concept for structural changes in the demand for money. If such changes are viewed as a reaction to a previously excessive money supply, it may be necessary to counter this development by means of corresponding reductions in the monetary target in order to 'normalise' the velocity of circulation – something which the Bundesbank attempted to do in 1980 and 1981. The situation is different in the case of exogenous changes in the demand for money which could stem from the increased use of Deutsche Mark (DM) bank notes abroad, or from a disproportionately large increase in the 'underground economy', where a large amount of cash is involved. It is becoming increasingly clear that there is a negative trend – amounting to around 0.5 per cent per annum – in the velocity of circulation of the central bank money stock with respect to the GNP (see Figure 3.2).

In view of the increasing automation and rationalisation of payment transactions, and the use of new payment media ('eurocheque', 'Eurocard'), however, this is difficult to explain. Particular attention will therefore have to be devoted in future to establishing whether this trend component is to be taken into account in the targets. This in any case gives rise to the question as to whether long-term discrepancies between money supply and money demand – provided that they develop gradually and steadily – can represent a problem for the economy at all, as it can be assumed that the private sector is sufficiently flexible in this respect.

During the first few years of the money stock concept, the Bundesbank attempted to realise the money stock projection directly in the form of a specific pinpointed target. Such a course means that monetary-policy action is subject to extremely rigid limitations. The central bank forgoes from the outset the opportunity to react to exogenous disturbances (for example, oil price shocks, major changes in the real exchange rate, abrupt cyclical fluctuations) which can always occur during a target period after the target has been announced. In such a case, the central bank's only choice is to adhere – against its better judgement – to a target course derived on the basis of assumptions which have in retrospect proved to be incorrect, or deliberately to fail to achieve the set target, something which requires a considerable amount of explaining to the public, and in the long run

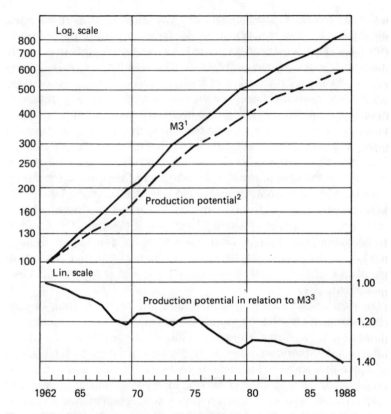

Figure 3.2   West German money stock M3 and production potential,
1962–88
Notes: 1. Adjusted for statistical breaks.
       2. Production potential projected with prices for the Gross Domestic
       Product.
       3. The calculation of production potential in relation to M3 is based
       on (1962 = 100).

Source: Monthly Reports of the Deutsche Bundesbank.

could also impair the credibility of the monetary strategy. It was
above all the experiences in 1978, a year which saw a substantial
increase in the value of the Deutsche Mark in real terms, and clear
overshooting of the money stock target, that prompted the Bundesbank to lay down its target from then on in the form of a target range
(from fourth quarter to fourth quarter). In many cases it opted to
specify, at the time the target range was announced, the conditions

which would play the decisive role in determining whether efforts were to be made to achieve the upper or lower limit of the range. In this respect the target ranges do not represent a return to a purely discretionary policy. What is involved here instead is a 'conditional rule', with the participants in the market already being told *ex ante* what form the 'feedback' between new information on macroeconomic data and the central bank's adaptation measures is to take. However, the Bundesbank has thereby also given itself a certain amount of scope for a moderately anticyclical policy.

3.3 INDIRECT CONTROL OF THE CENTRAL BANK MONEY STOCK

In implementing its strategy of monetary targeting the Bundesbank has opted, not for direct monetary base control of the type advocated by monetarists, but rather for indirect control of the central bank money stock via interest rate and liquidity policy. If a direct control technique were used, the central bank would make available to the commercial banks *pro rata temporis* the quantity of central bank money appropriate for achieving the target – primarily through open market operations in the form of minimum interest rate tenders – and accept the resultant interest rate effects without restriction. Instruments such as lombard loans which give the banks uncontrolled access to the supply of central bank money would have no place in such a control concept.[3]

Given the conditions still prevailing in West Germany today, however, such a course of action would not be readily possible: for individual banks, it is not only their central bank balances but also interbank balances which serve as the basis for liquidity, and at the same time as the basis for lending. On account of the minimum reserve calculation procedure used in West Germany, the extent of the central bank money requirements of the entire banking system in a particular month is not known until the second half of the month. From then on the banking system's demand for central bank money is to a large extent inelastic. As, moreover, no excess reserves are kept under the West German system, the Bundesbank has no choice for this short period other than to meet the banks' central bank money requirements. If instead – as a form of direct control – it were to adhere systematically to a specified money supply in the short run, there would certainly be a considerable increase in the day-to-day money rate, but this could not effect any liquidity equalisation, as in the case of a rigidly predetermined central bank money supply there can no longer be an appreciable reduction in demand even with rising money market rates. It would then be impossible to preclude the situation described by Horst Bockelmann as follows: 'Someone is caught between the two leaves of a closing door. Who it is has in case of doubt little to do with the business policy of these banks'.[4] Under such circumstances it would, in the final analysis, be only a matter of chance whether the banks comply with their minimum reserve requirements or not. If such a situation were to become the rule, the minimum reserve obligation itself might possibly lose some of its binding character for the banks.

In opposition to this argument it could be said that in the event of direct money stock control by the Bundesbank the banks would probably – in the course of time – go over to keeping sizeable excess reserves, as this would yield high interest earnings, at least to start with, for banks with a surplus. This, however, would involve a fundamental change in the system, something which the Bundesbank has not considered necessary to date. If the Bundesbank is 'subject to the pull of the banks' even for a short time with the system of indirect money stock control, this by no means implies that it would be impossible to control the development of the central bank money stock in accordance with the targets over somewhat longer periods. As the Bundesbank's monetary-policy instruments allow it to exert direct influence on the terms applying on the money market, it is in its power to influence the banks' lending decisions and 'liability management' in this way and thus also to influence the future extent of the banks' central bank money requirements. On the whole, this 'indirect' control of the central bank money stock has to date proved effective, although insufficient attention has been devoted to establishing how far this indirect control should actually go. It has so far remained open whether the central bank should lay down a specific interest level for the money market. Alternatively, another way of effecting 'indirect' control would be for the central bank to specify an *interest range*, with the rate for advances on securities (the lombard rate) acting as the upper limit and the discount rate as the lower limit. If such a strategy were employed, it would also have to be established what the practice would be – within this range – for securities repurchase agreements. In the more recent past money market control has been effected especially with the allotment rate for these transactions.

In the course of 1985, the volume of securities repurchase agreements, which had been used more and more as what might be called an instrument of 'fine tuning', that is, for limited periods of time, and within highly restricted quantitative limits, was expanded to a considerable degree. At a total of around DM 20 to 30 billion, such transactions today represent the most important source – next to rediscounting – for the permanent provision of central bank money. The advantage of this instrument, which is used in the form of a minimum interest rate or fixed interest rate tender, is that it allows money market terms – through both the funds supplied and the rates charged – to be controlled in a far more flexible manner than is possible with the traditional rediscounting and lombard loans.

3.4 RECENT EXPERIENCES WITH THE STRATEGY OF MONETARY TARGETING

If we consider the targets and the actual development of the central bank money stock, it becomes apparent that during the initial years of the concept's use, when a pinpointed target was still employed, the Bundesbank was unable to control the central bank money stock in accordance with the targets set. Whereas the target was missed by only 1 percentage point in 1976 and 1977, it was overshot by 2 percentage points in 1975, and in 1978, taking the average for the year, the central bank money stock was no less than 3.4 percentage points above the target course. The period from 1979 to 1985 presents a far better picture. Despite unfavourable and, in part, unforeseeable circumstances in terms of both foreign trade and payments and the domestic economy, it was possible every year to keep within the target ranges laid down from 1979 onwards (see Table 3.1). The accuracy of the control mechanism during this phase is demonstrated not least by the fact that it also proved possible every time to realise the more specifically defined target course announced half-way through the year. However, this positive trend did not continue in 1986. With the central bank money stock actually expanding by 7.7 per cent, the 1986 target range of 3.5–5.5 per cent was exceeded to a considerable extent (based on the mean potential-oriented value of 4.5 per cent, by 3.2 percentage points).

Leaving aside 1975, the first year in which the money stock concept was used, major deviations from the target really occurred only in 1978 and 1986. At first glance these two years exhibit a number of

Table 3.1   West German monetary targets and their implementation, 1975–89 (%)

| Year | Target growth of the central bank money stock | | Actual growth (rounded figures) | | Target achieved |
	In the course of the year[1]	On an annual average	In the course of the year[1]	On an annual average	
1975	8	–	10	–	no
1976	–	8	–	9	no
1977	–	8	–	9	no
1978	–	8	–	11	no
1979	6–9	–	6	–	yes
1980	5–8	–	5	–	yes
1981	4–7	–	4	–	yes
1982	4–7	–	6	–	yes
1983	4–7	–	7	–	yes
1984	4–6	–	5	–	yes
1985	3–5	–	5	–	yes
1986	$3\frac{1}{2}$–$5\frac{1}{2}$	–	8	–	no
1987	3–6	–	8	–	no
1988 (M3)	3–6	–	7	–	no
1989 (M3)	ca. 5	–	5	–	yes

[1] Between fourth quarter of the previous year and fourth quarter of the current year; 1975: December 1974 to December 1975.

similarities as regards the general economic situation which have frequently fostered the impression of parallel developments, at the same time suggesting that the policy of monetary targeting is vulnerable to external influences, and that during periods of low inflation rates and large current account surpluses the Bundesbank is more prepared to tolerate the stability-policy risks which overshooting of the target involves. However, it would be too simple a solution to base a diagnosis on presumed parallels between 1978 and 1986, an assumed 'benign neglect' attitude or a change of paradigm in monetary policy in favour of orientation towards exchange rates. The development of the monetary aggregates witnessed in 1986 is above all the reflection of a probably unparalleled overall economic situation.

In 1986 the Deutsche Mark increased in value by 35 per cent against the US dollar by comparison with the previous year (in 1978 the increase was 15.7 per cent); this corresponds to a real increase of 32.2

per cent in the value of the Deutsche Mark (1978: 10.3 per cent). For the first time since 1953 the inflation rate was negative, with consumer prices falling in 1986 by 0.2 per cent in comparison with 1985 (in 1978 prices had risen by 2.7 per cent). At DM 76.5 billion West Germany's current account surplus reached a new record level (1978 current account surplus: DM 18 billion), which was far higher than any figure achieved in the past, and only slightly lower than the cumulative current account surplus of DM 83.3 billion recorded for the whole of the post-war period up to the end of 1985. 1986 also saw a hitherto unequalled surplus in the balance of long-term capital transactions, amounting to some DM 38 billion. Although the domestic non-banks invested a net total of DM 42 billion abroad in the form of short-term financial and commercial credits, there was, nevertheless, still an exceptionally large externally-induced influx of liquid assets to be held by economic units in West Germany. Interest rates, which on the capital market had still been as high as 6.4 per cent at the beginning of 1986, fell to 5.6 per cent by April, and thus temporarily equalled the all-time low experienced in the spring of 1978.

Together with the replacement of foreign-currency holdings abroad with the Deutsche Mark, an event which was stimulated not least by revaluation expectations, the fact that the opportunity costs of holding liquid assets were low under these circumstances promoted a substantial increase in the volume of currency in circulation. The negative inflation rate meant that even non-interest-bearing sight deposits yielded a real return; savings deposits – the nominal interest on which had in the past generally been insufficiently geared to the price trend – produced a fairly high real interest yield by comparison with other interest-bearing assets. This too boosted the clear preference for near-money investments with banks (with comparatively little monetary capital formation). As the readiness to acquire long-term securities at the same time remained somewhat limited in view of the low nominal return on fixed-interest securities and interest rate increases generally expected by the market, a situation resulted which corresponded roughly to the model case of the Keynesian liquidity trap. In the investment of the externally-induced net influx of liquid resources, preference was likewise given to assets which are included in the money stock M3 and thus affect minimum reserves. The major influx of funds from abroad not only promoted the growth of monetary holdings, but also curbed domestic borrowing. Lending by the banking system (including the Bundesbank) to the domestic non-bank public increased by only 4 per cent in 1986 and was thus remarkably low (compared with the expansion of monetary aggregates, particularly the 8 per cent increase in required minimum reserves). However, another factor which probably also had an effect – possibly an even greater one – was the fact that many companies, not least on account of a sustained favourable earnings situation, had large liquidity 'cushions' at their disposal and that the propensity to invest declined substantially in the course of 1986.

Although the Central Bank Council of the Deutsche Bundesbank had still considered it likely in the first half of the year that the central bank money stock could be brought back into line with the target range, the development of this aggregate then accelerated. It is true that, in a system featuring flexible exchange rates and a flexible interest rate and liquidity policy on the part of the central bank, the expansion of the money stock can in principle be kept within acceptable narrow limits even in the event of large influxes of funds from abroad. In the special situation facing it, however, the Bundesbank had not only to bear in mind that the traditional reaction to excessive expansion of the monetary aggregates – which involves making it more expensive for banks to obtain funds from the central bank to finance their business – could induce further rapidly growing inflows of funds from abroad as a result of falling interest differentials and continuing revaluation expectations. When making its decisions the Bundesbank had also to take into account the retarding influences on economic growth in West Germany caused by the substantial increase in the value of the Deutsche Mark, particularly against the dollar. Other factors which it had to consider were the role of the Deutsche Mark as the second most important reserve and investment currency after the dollar and – last but by no means least – the considerable political pressure from the United States for solidarity in support of measures to stabilise exchange rates. In this situation the Bundesbank adopted what was more or less a wait-and-see attitude. It adhered to the monetary status quo; by thus meeting the demand for central bank money resulting from the development of bank deposits and the volume of currency in circulation, it refrained from active control of the expansion of the monetary aggregates.

When the situation within the European Monetary System (EMS) started to show signs of reaching crisis point towards the end of the year, the Bundesbank was unwilling – in view of the already accelerating monetary expansion – to support the weak member currencies through intramarginal intervention and interest-rate measures; it was expecting that there would be a realignment in any case and opted on 12 November 1986 for a minimum interest rate tender, which pushed up money-market interest rates to a small extent, rather than for a fixed interest rate tender of the type which had hitherto been preferred for many months. Once the lower intervention points (and accordingly the upper intervention points in the case of the Deutsche Mark and the Dutch guilder) in the EMS had been reached, the Bundesbank was obliged to purchase foreign currencies on a large scale (DM 17 billion). The realignment of 12 January 1987, which was realised more or less under protest, particularly on the part of France, involved a 3 per cent increase in the value of the Deutsche Mark (with respect to the central rates) and was insufficiently effective in that it did not – as had previously always been the case – result in a simple change of the positions of the currencies in the 'new' spread. By contrast with developments in the past, there was consequently likewise no immediate outflow of funds which had been transferred to West Germany for reasons of speculation. Although the Bundesbank allowed due securities repurchase agreements to expire without follow-up agreements, which quickly reduced the volume of such transactions from DM 34 billion to DM 18 billion, the central bank money stock continued to expand – admittedly more slowly, but nevertheless still to a greater extent than was desired. The same applied to the monetary holdings of non-banks.

The situation called for a monetary-policy reaction which had to involve both a reduction in money-market interest rates and an increase in the volume of securities repurchase agreements. The sensational package of measures adopted by the Bundesbank on 22 January 1987 indeed combined restrictive liquidity-related elements (reduction of the rediscount quota by DM 8 billion and a 10 per cent linear increase in the minimum reserve ratios) with cuts of 0.5 per cent in both the discount and lombard rates which lowered them to 3 per cent and 5 per cent respectively. We must nevertheless ask whether the decision taken was appropriate to the situation in terms of both the instruments chosen and the way in which their use was proportioned. The answer to this question must above all take into account the fact that the Bundesbank can control the monetary aggregates only indirectly by laying down monetary data, waiting to see how the market reacts to them and then correcting them again. We are thus dealing with a virtually endless process of action and reaction which is nevertheless more than just a simple process of trial and error. The principal monetary authority – the Central Bank

Council – is always guided in its decisions by carefully prepared conceptions regarding monetary-policy configurations which are in line with the monetary and general economic situation at a particular time; however, only the processes of adaptation which they trigger on the market can show whether or not they are truly appropriate to the situation. Adequate flexibility in the use of monetary-policy instruments, not least the refinancing rates, is essential if these processes are to be anticipated reasonably accurately, and if it is to be possible to react quickly and effectively to changes of all types on the market – always, of course, in fundamental harmony with the basic strategic positions of monetary policy.

Some years ago the Central Bank Council had already been concerned to see that neither the discount rate nor the lombard rate could be used as flexibly as the monetary situation at the time would in principle have required. It was above all the desire for continuity in monetary-policy configurations, and thus the adherence for long periods to basic interest rates fixed at some point in the past, that fostered a trend in public opinion which interpreted every change in the two interest rates as a change of direction in monetary policy; the anticipation of likely and in most cases undesired reactions on the part of the banks and the non-bank public meant that there was even greater inflexibility in the use of these monetary-policy instruments. Instead of restricting the difference between the two basic interest rates to around half a percentage point, therefore, a measure which would normally have been advisable and which had also been considered by the Central Bank Council, it was decided in February 1985 to increase the gap to 1.5 percentage points. This was associated with the declared intention[5] of also utilising this scope in monetary-policy terms in order – among other things – to prepare the way for changes in basic interest rates. Securities repurchase agreements became the most important instrument of 'fine tuning'. However, the policy of controlling money-market interest rates within the spread emerged in the form of a type of monetary management which endeavoured in every situation to minimise interest-rate fluctuations on money markets as far as possible. This was achieved through a preference for fixed interest rate tenders in the case of securities repurchase agreements, whose allotment rate thus assumed the function of a basic interest rate by way of substitution, accompanied by a treasury bill selling rate as a lower safeguarding line, and by further operations on the money market, for example, through the transfer of Federal and *Land* Government funds in accordance with Article 17 of the Bundesbank Act, or swaps on the foreign exchange market. As a result the day-to-day money rates exhibited a form of development which, leaving aside brief deviations, can more or less be described as representing a 'snake' in the 'interest tunnel' (see Figure 3.3). In monetary-policy terms, such a course of action, with interest rates remaining largely constant for lengthy periods as was the case in 1986, for example, implies that the demand for central bank money at any given time is met almost unreservedly and that there is therefore, *de facto*, no active indirect control of the expansion of monetary aggregates. Monetary policy, which all money theorists agree must ultimately be supply-oriented irrespective of the techniques used, thereby develops a strong bias towards the demand side. Moreover, 'fine tuning' which is structured in this way comes very close to being a form of official monetary-policy control if it is linked with conceptions regarding the correct exchange rate or possible cyclical policy stimuli.

In addition to boosting the volume of securities repurchase agreement, which play a key role in this context, the principal effect of the measures adopted on 22 January 1987 was a cut of half a percentage point in central-bank interest rates. Efforts were also made, through ample provision of bank liquidity, to ensure that very short-term money-market rates – contrary to the situation that had prevailed for the most part in 1986 – were kept below the 3.8 per cent allotment rate for fixed interest rate tenders. This form of monetary management, of course, finds favour with money managers in particular, who thereby see themselves relieved of numerous risks and thus also of many worries. However, the necessary reliance on continuity in monetary policy also involves the freedom and the obligation to react to undesirable trends in monetary aggregates and to changes in the situation on financial markets.

The demand for greater flexibility in monetary management speaks in favour – among other things – of the minimum interest rate tender; seen in these terms, such tenders should be given basic priority over the fixed interest rate tender, although preference will undoubtedly have to be given to the latter in certain situations. However, it has still to be established whether the minimum interest rate tender is to continue to be used as has been the case to date (allotment at a uniform interest rate of which notice is given in advance), or whether the American method (allotment of the proportionate quotas at the interest rate appropriate in each case) is more advisable. In the case of a fixed interest rate tender, moreover, it is by no means a matter of

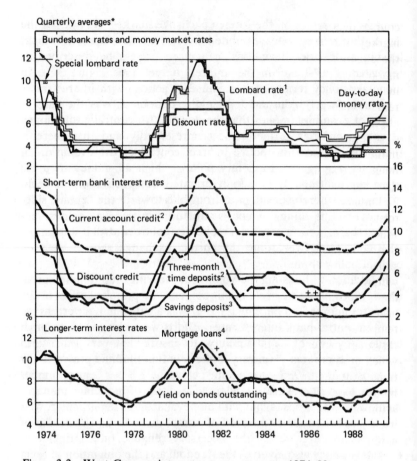

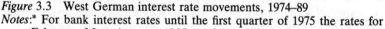

Figure 3.3   West German interest rate movements, 1974–89

*Notes:** For bank interest rates until the first quarter of 1975 the rates for
February, May, August and November.
1. From 1 June 1973 to 3 July 1974 and from 20 February 1981 to 6 May
1982 lombard loans were not granted at the lombard rate; during these
periods (for the first time on 26 November 1973) the Bundesbank
provided special lombard loans at a special lombard rate as and when
required.
2. Of less than DM 1 million.
3. At statutory notice.
4. On residential real estate, effective rate of interest.
+ From June 1982, only average rate for floating-rate mortgage loans;
data comparable with earlier figures only to a limited extent.
++ From June 1986, rate for time deposits from DM 100,000 to less
than DM 1 million.

course that additional operations will always 'push' the money-market rate to the level where it actually ought to be in the opinion of those concerned with monetary policy; in this way, informative market reactions are sterilised in their early stages. Lastly, there are many indications that in normal circumstances the treasury bill selling rate should not be used as the lower limit for interest-rate fluctuations. Undesirable interest-rate trends can be countered with the aid of other monetary-policy instruments; the close links with the Euro-money markets also help to ensure (partially) compensatory flows of financial resources. Seen in these terms, it does not appear certain that the package of measures adopted by the Bundesbank on 22 January 1987 was really optimal. The same applies to the liquidity-related measures in the narrower sense of the term, the application of which has not been particularly convincing. It must be emphasised that a monetary policy which reacts more flexibly to the given situation on money markets will bring with it sizeable fluctuations within – and for brief periods possibly beyond – the spread whose limits are marked by the discount rate and the lombard rate. It may also be the case that interest-rate movements of this type will have a temporary effect on the exchange rate. However, any form of monetary management geared to exchange rates or current cyclical data which endeavours to prevent supposedly unacceptable market reactions contains an inherent conflict with the aim of controlling the money stock. It should never be forgotten in this connection that stabilisation of the development of the central bank money stock in itself already helps to stabilise the business cycle to a considerable extent.

The major concern of monetary policy must nevertheless be to remain calculable and trustworthy.[6] This requires a clear conceptual orientation and this is provided by a medium-term potential-oriented strategy of monetary targeting. Such a strategy is based on the causal relationship between changes in the money stock and the price trend, a relationship which should in principle be beyond all doubt. It also takes account of the monetarist imperative which states that as a result of inadequate knowledge of the interrelationships, and because of long and variable lags, a discretionary monetary policy will create more instabilities in the private sector than it can eliminate. The complex links between the development of monetary aggregates, particularly the central bank money stock, and changes in the price level,[7] involving in some cases very long lags (between six and eleven quarters), have encouraged false hope that the present situation, characterised by sustained excessive expansion of monetary aggregates and *de facto* price stability, is an indication that the fundamental causality has ceased to exist, at least for the time being, or – in the light of external influences – is more or less being reversed. The determination of lags using econometric methods in this field is of little use in that it is always the prevailing situation which determines whether the causal relationship has a rapid or less rapid effect. At present, it is above all the price-curbing effects of a major improvement in the terms of trade (1986: +15.3 per cent) which have more than neutralised other price-raising factors which still exist. 1987 is likely to witness inflationary pressures once more, at least from the cost side. Moreover, renewed expectations of inflation are also sufficient to generate demand in the economy as a whole as arrangements are made regarding assets.

3.5 PROSPECTS

But how can monetary policy become more efficient? Is it likely that the scope for monetary-policy action will become greater once again? Will the now substantially changed international economic situation and the general conditions in the European monetary sector make it possible to continue to pursue a medium-term strategy of monetary targeting, geared to West Germany's domestic economic situation, in order to achieve the goal of price stability? Given the current international economic situation, the Bundesbank will also be obliged this year to find an appropriate balance between domestic and external economic requirements. However, this is not due – as is so often maintained – solely to the globalisation of financial markets and thus to the internationalisation of financial links. These factors represent necessary, but nevertheless insufficient, conditions. An equally important role has been played by the special state of affairs already mentioned. West Germany's capital transactions with other countries have after all been fully liberalised for many years now; a situation comparable to that in 1986 had nevertheless not been experienced hitherto. It is likewise inappropriate to view the so-called 'monetary innovations' as the decisive factor. The basic institutional conditions (abolition of all interest-rate controls as far back as 1967 and a flexible universal bank system) and the general macroeconomic conditions (a high degree of price stability and relatively small fluctuations in market interest rates) have done practically nothing in West

Germany to occasion the large-scale introduction of a succession of financial innovations. The 'residual liberalisation' which took place in May 1985 has likewise not played a role of any major significance. Considerably greater importance must be attached to the expectations with regard to changes in interest-rate levels and exchange rates as well as in the Bundesbank's monetary-policy stance. The Bundesbank must bear in mind above all that any abandonment of potential-oriented monetary-policy action, for example, on account of foreign policy considerations, can very easily create the impression of a permissive monetary policy – which is in any case being pursued in many countries today – and thus also encourages expectations of inflation. It is therefore essential to make consistent use of scope for monetary-policy action wherever it exists. Above all, it is important to counter the suspicion that the Bundesbank is simultaneously pursuing – with a greater or lesser degree of success – a monetary target, targets for interest rates, cyclical targets and – at the latest after the Louvre conference – an exchange rate target, albeit of a 'weak' variety. As such target variables are incompatible with one another, the Bundesbank would have no option in the event of a conflict – which virtually always exists – other than to fail to achieve one or even two of these 'targets', which would inevitably give rise to public doubts as to the quality of monetary policy. A central bank should simply never arouse hopes that its monetary policy will allow it to pursue targets for which its resources are unsuitable or inadequate; it should aim still less to realise such a complex set of targets.

Every central bank, particularly one with such a high international standing as the Bundesbank, must, of course, take account of the general international economic situation. This is characterised today by a desire for greater exchange rate stability, even though arguments are usually based on national viewpoints and 'convenient' demands made on other countries. Even the measures which are urgently required in view of the weakness of the dollar and are presented in the guise of international solidarity are no exception to the rule.

In a detailed study produced in 1984, the International Monetary Fund[8] came to the conclusion that more stable exchange rates can only be achieved in a system of flexible exchange rates if all countries simultaneously pursue a stable, credible and balanced economic policy. One attempt to introduce rules for economic-policy 'convergence' at international level is represented by the list of ten 'objective indicators'[9] adopted by countries participating in the 1986

World Economic Summit in Tokyo. These indicators are intended to reveal inconsistent economic policies at an early stage, occasion the adjustment of economic policies, and show whether the countries are in general pursuing a policy which is too restrictive or too expansive. However, it has not yet been established how deviations of the indicators are to be weighted or how they are to be corrected. The success or failure of the concept – and of any form of monetary co-operation – will in the final analysis be determined by the extent to which the participating countries are prepared to respect the rules which it involves. This also applies in principle to exchange-rate 'target zones'[10] or less ambitious declarations of intent where – for example – the countries involved are required to intervene on foreign exchange markets in a co-ordinated manner when specific exchange rates are reached. Strict orientation towards rules inherent in the system is even more of a *sine qua non* for all further developed proposed solutions bearing a similarity to a system of fixed exchange rates. Such as the concept put forward by McKinnon,[11] who envisages that national money stock control should be replaced by joint control of the world money stock by the Federal Reserve, the Bundesbank and the Bank of Japan, along with specific target zones for exchange rates. Changes in money stocks and interest rates are intended to stabilise exchange rates within the target zones. However, econometric studies which have examined exchange rate trends over the past ten to fifteen years do not indicate that there is any statistically proven link between the development of the money stock (as well as the interest-rate trend) and the development of exchange rates. The 'target zone' concept thus involves the major risk that monetary policy will be used to stabilise exchange rates and will therefore come into conflict with its domestic objectives without the desired end actually being achieved. There are many indications that all concepts currently under discussion for reforming the international monetary order, with their more or less marked incorporation of features of a fixed-rate system, would fail on account of their lack of conclusiveness *in concreto* in view of the immense and still rapidly expanding financial markets. These concepts are mere half measures; they are in essence incongruent conglomerations of institutional provisions, internally inconsistent target conceptions, inadequate sets of instruments, and in the long run non-binding behaviour rules. As things stand, it is at all events better for the time being to place hopes in economic-policy convergence and in effective co-operation between central banks wherever this is appropriate.

The situation within the European Monetary System is somewhat different. After many years of rigid confrontation between the viewpoints of monetarists and post-Keynesians, there has now been a *rapprochement*. It has become generally accepted that the start of a process of more extensive integration in the monetary sector must be marked, not by institutional regulations, but by the 'fusing' of financial markets and convergence in terms of monetary policy. In accordance with the decision of the European Council (Article 8a of the Single European Act), a 'large internal market', which is also to have a 'financial dimension',[12] is to be realised by 1992 in the Community countries. If this declaration is taken literally, it implies above all the totally unhindered movement of 'financial products' across national frontiers, which in turn would necessitate unrestricted, and in the long run irreversible, abolition of all capital movement controls, at least within Europe. If, however, market forces can react quickly and effectively to diverging economic developments (which would be the case in such a market), the problem of the burden-sharing inherent in the system – a problem which must be solved in the EMS just as it must in any fixed-rate system – would become particularly important. If the burden is to be borne out by primarily strong-currency countries, they would find themselves with even greater obligations than before, with the danger that the integration target of the internal European market would then be in conflict, for example, with the Bundesbank's stability mandate. If, however, the rules are designed such that the less stable countries in particular are forced to adapt their economic policies to the stability-oriented countries, further integration of financial markets would then improve the system's macroeconomic functioning – at least from the traditional German viewpoint. In other European countries, however, this would also inevitably increase the already more or less openly expressed indignation at a hegemony on the part of the Deutsche Mark and the Deutsche Bundesbank's stability policy geared primarily to domestic economic goals.[13]

Indeed, as soon as the first steps have been taken towards liberalisation of capital markets, particularly in France, the expected consequences are being anticipated and demands made in the light of these for closer monetary co-operation more or less as a preliminary to unrestricted financial markets. Early co-ordination of monetary-policy action is to be achieved by means of co-ordinated monetary-policy objectives and increased gearing of diagnosis and practical action to the divergence indicators as an expression of diverging overall developments. In the event of strains on foreign exchange markets it is envisaged that there should be joint intramarginal intervention, where possible with recourse to the EMS support regulations (credit facilities); interest-policy measures are also to be agreed upon, likewise in an effort to prevent realignments where possible. In order to reduce the pressure on other European countries caused by major changes in the exchange rate between the Deutsche Mark and the dollar, co-ordinated intervention is recommended relating not just to the US dollar and the Deutsche Mark, but also to other currencies, above all the French franc. This would, *de facto*, give rise to forms of monetary co-operation which approximate to the functional conditions of the 'basket solution' in the EMS. West German monetary policy would be integrated into an interlinked European set-up, and in so far could no longer be so systematically geared to domestic economic circumstances in West Germany as has been the case hitherto. The position of the Deutsche Mark would thereby be modified; the other participating currencies would then, at least in principle, have the chance of achieving equal status, above all if – as is currently the case in France – the countries in question pursue a consistent stabilisation policy in preparation for the transition from a weak national currency to a strong one. The European Currency Unit (ECU) – contrary to the situation which has prevailed in recent years – plays a somewhat secondary role in this context. West Germany will not simply be able to ignore the demands of its partners in the EMS; it will have to ask itself what it can offer in the way of additional co-operation without jeopardising or indeed abandoning the core of its stability-oriented policy. To implement measures such as the merging of the private and official ECU circuits, or unlimited access to credit facilities in the case of intramarginal intervention, would be to cross the Rubicon; this would not apply, however, to steps such as allowing West German residents to hold ECU accounts at West German credit institutions, or introducing optional co-operation in the case of intervention within the margin.

The globalisation of financial markets and the structural changes on domestic markets generally referred to as 'financial innovations', have led to changes in the general conditions surrounding West German monetary policy. However, an even greater impact is being created by increasingly significant political intentions which are now starting to take shape within the EMS, although not so much in the international context. The Bundesbank, like all central banks, must face up to the challenges confronting it today.

Appendix 3.1 Calculation procedure for determining the Deutsche Bundesbank's monetary target

The target is derived on the basis of the Deutsche Bundesbank's views with regard to the desired economic development during the year in question.

For the targets for the years up to and including 1984 the following factors were taken into account:

(a) the expected growth in the production potential.
(b) the desirable change in the utilisation of the production potential.
(c) the 'unavoidable' rise in prices.
(d) the expected development of the 'velocity of circulation' of money.

With price stability having been achieved to a large extent by the end of 1984, it became unnecessary to take the 'unavoidable increase in prices' into account.

For 1986 the money stock target was derived as stated below. The following were taken as the basis:

– Real growth of the production potential + 2.5 per cent
– Rise in the overall price level, measured by the GNP deflator + 2 per cent
– Increase in the production potential at current prices + 4.5 per cent
Targets: Average expansion of central bank money stock during the year + 4.5 per cent
Rate of change from 4th quarter of 1985 to 4th quarter of 1986 + 4.0–4.5 percent
Target range + 3.5–5.5 per cent
Note: No allowance was made for changes in the utilisation of the production potential and the velocity of circulation, as purely cyclical fluctuations in the utilisation of the production potential are matched by similar changes in the velocity of circulation and there is no sign of a change in the trend as regards cash-holding habits.

Appendix 3.2 The Bundesbank's Monetary Policy since 1988

After the central bank money stock (CBMS) had again exceeded its target substantially in 1987, the Central Bank Council was confronted with the difficult task to formulate the monetary target for 1988. One option recommended by a group of economists inside and outside the Council was a strategy based on several indicators (CBMS, M1, M3, domestic credit) instead of a single target aggregate, thereby generally reducing the political importance of the monetary target. Another possibility was a monetary policy without any pre-announced target. The Council, nevertheless, did not change its overall policy strategy although it was clear that dilemma situations might occur again, where the monetary target conflicts with the EMS obligations or international agreements to stabilise exchange rates. The decision to continue the concept of monetary targeting was based on the experience since 1973. It has been evident that the target stands as a symbol of the Bundesbank's resolve to defend the value of money even if there is a

Table 3A.1   Weights of West Germany's main components in M3 and the central bank money stock (CBMS) and their relative share (end of 1987)

Components	CBMS		M3	
	weight	share (in %)	weight	share (in %)
Currency in circulation	1	50.9	1	11.2
Sight deposits	0.166	16.8	1	23.5
Time deposits	0.124	13.7	1	23.3
Savings deposits	0.081	18.6	1	42.0

conflict with other policy targets. The announcement of the target is a demonstration to the public that the Bundesbank is setting itself under a burden of proof if the money supply exceeds the targeted value. Thus, although the Council saw the risks for the Bundesbank's credibility, it expected a much greater threat to its reputation if it switched to a completely discretionary policy regime.

The monetary target for 1988 differs from the targets since 1975 as it is expressed in terms of the broad money stock M3, which comprises currency plus sight deposits, time deposits for less than four years, and savings deposits at statutory notice held with domestic banks. Thus, the M3 aggregate is made up of almost the same monetary components as the CBMS, which is defined as the sum of currency in circulation plus required reserves on domestic deposits (calculated at constant reserve ratios, base: January 1974). The two indicators differ mainly by their weighting of these components (see Table 3.A1), which results in very different percentage shares especially of the currency component.[14]

The strong influence of the demand for bank notes and coins on the development of the central bank money stock was the main reason for the overexpansion of this monetary aggregate in 1987. From the fourth quarter of 1986, to the fourth quarter of 1987, the reserve component of the CBMS rose by only 5.8 per cent, while the currency component increased by 10.3 per cent. In the same period M3 grew at a rate of 6.1 per cent which would have been still in accordance with the upper limit of the target for 1987 (3–6 per cent).

Except for these short-term divergencies, the CBMS and M3 have moved broadly in parallel over the last fifteen years on account of their similar definitions. In addition, the econometric results for money demand functions with M3 or CBMS reveal rather identical statistical properties of both aggregates.[15] Therefore, with its new target aggregate the Bundesbank wants to reduce the influence of disruptive factors (for example, demand for Deutsche Mark currency in situations of a Deutsche Mark appreciation against the dollar) on its monetary policy.

In spite of the new definition, the revised monetary target was not reached in 1988. In the first half of the year, the demand for money remained rather strong, mainly due to the lagged effects of interest rate cuts from the late autumn of 1987 and the increased holding of Deutsche Mark notes abroad.

In the second half of 1988, the introduction of a withholding tax for capital incomes scheduled for the beginning of the year 1989 lead to a downright 'flight' of German investors into cash. This financial shock, which significantly boosted the monetary expansion was accommodated by the Bundesbank. Thus, from the fourth quarter of 1987 to the fourth quarter of 1988, the money stock M3 grew at a rate of 6.7 per cent – slightly above the upper target range of 6 per cent.

For the year 1989, the monetary target was again formulated on the basis of the money stock M3. Instead of a corridor, the target was expressed as a point target of 'about 5 per cent'. The increased tightening of monetary conditions by the Bundesbank's monetary policy in the course of the year caused a considerable deceleration of monetary growth in 1989. In addition, the demand for money was weakened by the rapid abolition of the withholding tax in the first half of 1989. On the whole, from the fourth quarter of 1988 to the fourth quarter of 1989, the money stock M3 increased at a rate of 4.7 per cent. Thus, after three years of overshooting, the monetary target had been reached again.

The monetary target for 1991 was set as a 'corridor' of 4 per cent to 6 per cent. This reorientation to the practice of the period from 1979 to 1987 reflects the intention to harmonise the procedure for monetary targeting in Europe as a precondition for the enhanced European monetary policy co-ordination in stage one, which started on 1 July 1990. More leeway was also needed in order to cope with the uncertainties associated with the monetary and economic integration of West and East Germany.

Notes

1. Cf. Sachverständigenrat zur Begutachtung der gesamtwirtschaftlichen Entwicklung (Council of Economic Experts), 'Gleicher Rang für den Geldwert', in *Jahresgutachten 1972–3* (Stuttgart/Mainz, December 1972) sections 394–405.
2. For details see 'More Flexibility in the Money Market' *Report of the Deutsche Bundesbank for the Year 1985* (Frankfurt a.M., April 1986), pp. 35–8. See also Frowen and Schlomann, pp. 59–81, of this volume.
3. Cf. Sachverständigenrat zur Begutachtung der gesamtwirtschaftlichen Entwicklung, 'Mut zur Stabilisierung' in *Jahresgutachten 1973–4* (Stuttgart/Mainz, December 1973) section 171, and 'Vollbeschäftigung für morgen' *Jahresgutachten 1974–5* (Stuttgart/Mainz, December 1974) section p. 383.
4. 'Streitfragen zur Kontrolle der Geldschöpfung durch die Notenbank', in *Schriften des Vereins für Socialpolitik*, New Series, **99** (Berlin, 1978) 44.
5. For details see 'The Longer-term Trend and Control of the Money Stock', *Monthly Report of the Deutsche Bundesbank*, vol. 37, January 1985, pp. 13–26.
6. Regarding this problem cf. OECD Working Papers no. 39, 'Monetary Policy in the Second Half of the 1980s: How Much Room for Manoeuvre?', February 1987.
7. Cf. 'The Longer-term Trend and Control of the Money Stock, pp. 20 ff.;

K.-D. Geisler, 'Zur "Kausalität" von Geldmenge und Sozialprodukt', *Kredit und Kapital, 319* (1986) 325–38.

8. International Monetary Fund, *The Exchange Rate System: Lessons of the Past and Options for the Future*, Occasional Paper no. 30 (Washington, DC, July 1984).

9. Regarding co-ordination of economic policy on the basis of indicators cf. J. A. Baker, 'Statement before the Committee on Foreign Relations of the U.S. Senate', *U.S. Treasury News*, Washington, DC, 20 May 1986; 'Statement before the International Trade Subcommittee of the Senate .Finance Committee and the International Finance and Monetary Policy Subcommittee of the Senate Banking Committee', *U.S. Treasury news*, Washington, DC, 13 May 1986; 'The Functioning of the International Monetary System, Statement before the IMF Interim Committee', *U.S. Treasury News*, Washington, DC, 9–10 April 1986. J. Williamson, *Target Zones and Indicators as Instruments for International Economic Policy Coordination: A Report to the Group of 24* (Washington, DC, September 1986).

10. Regarding the 'target zone concept', see J. Williamson, *The Exchange Rate System*, Institute for International Economics, **5**, 2nd edn (Washington, DC, 1985); 'Target Zones and the Management of the Dollar', *Brookings Papers on Economic Activity*, **1** (1986) 165–75; *Exchange Rate Flexibility, Target Zones, and Policy Coordination* (Washington, DC, May 1986).

11. R. I. McKinnon, *An International Standard for Monetary Stabilization*, Institute for International Economics, **8** (Washington, DC, March 1984); *Monetary and Exchange Rate Policies for International Financial Stability: A Proposal* (Standford, California, September 1986); 'The Dollar Exchange Rate and International Monetary Cooperation', in R. Hafer, (ed.), *The Increasing Openness of the US Economy* (The Federal Reserve Bank of St. Louis, 1986) 211–31.

12. Cf. Commission of the European Communities, *Completion of the Internal Market*, Commission white paper to the European Council, doc. COM (85) 310 final of 14 June 1985, Luxembourg, June 1985. See also Wissenschaftlicher Beirat (Advisory Council) at the Federal Ministry for Economic Affairs, 'Stellungnahme zum Weißbuch der EG-Kommission über den Binnenmarkt', *Studienreihe*, **51** (published by the Federal Ministry for Economic Affairs).

13. For details cf. N. Kloten, 'Wege zu einer Europäischen Währungsunion – Chancen und Risiken', *Wirtschaftspolitische Kolloquien der Adolf-Weber-Stiftung*, **14** (Berlin 1987).

14. A minor difference exists with respect to the comparatively illiquid block of savings deposits at agreed notice of less than four years and bank savings bonds with maturities of less than four years; these are not included in M3 in contrast to the central bank money stock.

15. See 'The Longer-term Trend and Control of the Money Stock', *Monthly Report of the Deutsche Bundesbank*, vol. 37, January 1985 pp. 13–26.

4 Financial Innovations and the Stability of the Demand for Money in Germany since 1974[*]

Stephen F. Frowen and
Heinrich Schlomann

4.1 INTRODUCTION

The Federal Republic of Germany has experienced a stronger dependence on foreign money markets after a large increase in both domestic and foreign interest rates in the early 1970s. In this chapter we examine the effects of this stronger dependence on the stability of the demand for money in West Germany.

One must first find a suitable observation period for the analysis. Recent studies suggest that, towards the end of 1973, there was a structural break with regard to different definitions of the money stock. For example, Buscher (1984a, p. 533) found a structural break in the third quarter of 1973, but stressed at the same time that, from 1974 to the end of his study in 1982, the estimates were once again stable. Buscher and Schroeder (1983, p. 310) and Neumann (1983, p. 417), using different equations, came to the same conclusion, namely that in the third quarter of 1973 there was a structural break. Assuming that the stability hypothesis is not rejected by random fluctuations of the estimated parameters, Buscher was unable to show any instability of the parameter estimates (Buscher 1984b, p. 270 ff.).[1] Therefore this analysis begins with the first quarter of 1974 and ends with the first quarter of 1987. The information used was unadjusted and seasonally-adjusted monthly data from the West German central bank, the Deutsche Bundesbank. These values were then reduced to quarterly averages and the logarithms were used in the estimations. The basis of the analysis was the following model:[2,3]

$$\ln M_t = \beta_0 + \sum_{i=0}^{1} \beta_{1i} \ln M_{t-1-i} + \sum_{i=0}^{1} \beta_{2i} \ln Y_{t-i}$$

$$+ \sum_{i=0}^{1} \beta_{3i} \ln i_{M,\,t-i} + \sum_{i=0}^{1} \beta_{4i} \ln i_{b,\,t-i}$$

$$+ \sum_{i=0}^{1} \beta_{5i} \ln e_{t-i} + \sum_{i=0}^{1} \beta_{6i} \ln f_{t-i}$$

$$+ \sum_{i=0}^{1} \beta_{7i} \ln P_{t-i} + u_t$$

and

$$\ln(M/P)_t = \beta_0 + \sum_{i=0}^{1} \beta_{1i} \ln(M/P)_{t-1-i} + \sum_{i=0}^{1} \beta_{2i} \ln (Y/P)_{t-i}$$

$$+ \sum_{i=0}^{1} \beta_{3i} \ln i_{M,\,t-i} + \sum_{i=0}^{1} \beta_{4i} \ln i_{b,\,t-i}$$

$$+ \sum_{i=0}^{1} \beta_{5i} \ln e_{t-i} + \sum_{i=0}^{1} \beta_{6i} \ln f_{t-i} + u$$

with:
M = quantity of money M1, M2 or M3 as defined by the Deutsche Bundesbank (the terms quantity of money and money stock are used synonymously here)
Y = gross national product at nominal prices
i_M = the average interest rate for three-month credits on the Frankfurt money market
i_b = average interest yield on taxable bonds
e = US\$/DM exchange rate
f = US\$/DM forward rate
P = average price index for private households (1980 = 100)
u = residuals
t = time index

According to Keynesian theory, aggregate income as well as interest rates are the variables of greatest influence on the demand for money. From the neoclassical theory's point of view, money is only one possible form of asset holding. Thus for any long-run analysis the volume of wealth, too, must be considered as an influence on the demand for money.

In empirical analysis of the demand for money, the income variable has a central position, because it is seen as an indicator of the volume of transactions in the economy. The opportunity costs of holding money are included by means of interest rates obtainable on alternative assets. In our model, the interest rate of three-month credits in the Frankfurt money market is an indicator of short-term interest rates while the average interest yield on taxable bonds is used as an indicator of long-term interest rates.

The presence of the US$/DM exchange and forward rates in the model take care of any external influences. This enables us to model not only the actual relationship between the US$ and the Deutsche Mark, but also expected future rates of exchange. We decided against the inclusion of foreign interest rates into the model, as under the assumption of a complete mobility of the bond market such rates would simply be the difference between the domestic interest rate and the swap rate, which can in fact be calculated from the exchange rate and the forward rate.

Analysing the demand for money in the short run, the level of the expected demand for money is often calculated with the help of a partial adjustment model. This procedure assumes institutional obstructions in the money market and also allows for the fact that individuals cannot react spontaneously to economic changes. The model of partial adjustment of the expected demand for money to its actual value leads to the equations above, explaining the actual demand for money, where the lagged variable of the money stock is one of the exogenous variables.

For the nominal demand for money functions, the price level is included as an explanatory variable. If there is money illusion in the economy, the price level would have a significant influence on the demand for money of individuals.

The equations to determine the money stocks M1, M2 and M3 were estimated using unadjusted as well as seasonally adjusted data. Furthermore, nominal as well as real functions were used. To obtain indicators of possible instability, regressions were calculated for the periods 1974 to 1980 and 1981 to 1987 (first quarter) as well as for the entire period from 1974 to 1987 (first quarter). The results obtained are analysed below. The estimated values can be found in Tables 4.1 to 4.10. The estimates were calculated by SPSS on the data processing system of the University of Frankfurt.

4.2 THE SPECIFICATION OF SUITABLE DEMAND FOR MONEY FUNCTIONS

4.2.1 Regressions for the Quantity of Money M1

The important factors regarding nominal demand for money functions are (apart from the lagged money stock variable) the gross national product (GNP) of the period observed, the money market interest rate for the observed or previous period, the actual or lagged forward exchange rates and, when forward interest rates are considered, the price index. The interest rates, the exchange rate as well as the forward rates represent the opportunity costs of holding money, whereas the other variables are indicators of the transaction motive for holding cash. It turns out that the lagged money market interest rates exert a greater influence than the unlagged ones. A corresponding statement is not possible with regard to the forward rate. The inclusion of the price index, when unadjusted data is used, leads to a reduction of the estimated coefficients for the lagged money variable and the GNP variable and, in the case of seasonally adjusted functions, this leads to an implausible negative influence of the price level and a reduction of the influence of the GNP in favour of the lagged money variable. By comparison, using the unadjusted data, a larger influence of the GNP at the expense of the lagged money stock is stated. The combined influence of these highly correlated variables is about the same in both cases.

The adjusted R^2 ($\bar{R}^2$) is very high for both the original and the seasonally adjusted data, although the standard error for the seasonally adjusted data is considerably smaller than for the original data (about 0.8 per cent and 2.2 per cent respectively). Besides this, in two cases the absolute value of the h-statistic is considerably above 1.645, so that the hypothesis of first degree autocorrelation cannot be rejected (see Table 4.1). The h-statistic is asymptotically standard normally distributed, so that the hypothesis of no first-order autocorrelation can be rejected at the 5 per cent level provided $|h| > 1.645$. In this context it should be indicated that the t-statistic has to be used with caution because it is distorted if the supposition of autocorrelation cannot be rejected.

The results of the equations estimated in real terms (see Table 4.2) are similar, but the relevant influences determined here are largely different. In the unadjusted data, aside from the lagged money variable, the GNP and lagged forward rate as well as the actual or

Table 4.1 OLS-estimation results for the West German nominal demand for money: M1 (all logarithms)

	const.	M_{t-1}	Y_t	Y_{t-1}	$i_{M,t}$	$i_{M,t-1}$	$i_{b,t}$	$i_{b,t-1}$	e_t	f_t	f_{t-1}	P_t	$\bar{R}^2$	SEE	h
Seasonally unadjusted:															
1	-0.938	0.178 (2.12)	0.545 (7.53)		0.021 (0.77)	-0.084 (-2.79)				-0.146 (-4.17)		0.529 (2.76)	0.993	0.021	-0.828
2	-0.889	0.200 (2.56)	0.567 (8.54)			-0.062 (-6.53)				-0.141 (-4.12)		0.463 (2.71)	0.993	0.020	-0.929
3	-0.742	0.257 (3.56)	0.654 (10.46)			-0.063 (-6.39)					-0.136 (-4.16)	0.253 (1.75)	0.993	0.021	-1.497
4	-0.510	0.354 (7.48)	0.714 (13.42)		-0.053 (-6.40)						-0.092 (-4.40)		0.993	0.021	-1.861*
5	-0.504	0.374 (7.70)	0.690 (12.68)		-0.047 (-5.56)					-0.076 (-3.69)			0.992	0.022	-1.401
6	-0.692	0.297 (3.87)	0.635 (9.15)		-0.052 (-5.54)					-0.112 (-3.20)		0.210 (1.28)	0.992	0.022	-1.273
Seasonally adjusted:															
7	1.298	0.646 (14.88)		0.293 (4.73)	-0.045 (-12.68)					-0.063 (-4.62)		-0.207 (-2.71)	0.995	0.008	0.729
8	1.332	0.625 (12.81)	0.295 (4.36)		-0.044 (-12.27)					-0.064 (-5.04)		-0.193 (-2.42)	0.995	0.008	0.078
9	1.047	0.691 (16.24)		0.133 (6.77)	-0.044 (-11.68)					-0.077 (-5.80)			0.994	0.008	0.842
10	1.042	0.689 (12.93)	0.136 (5.45)		-0.047 (-9.69)						-0.077 (-4.52)		0.994	0.009	1.896*
11	1.065	0.682 (15.20)	0.138 (6.61)		-0.043 (-11.50)					-0.079 (-5.73)			0.994	0.009	0.732

Note: t-values in parenthesis.
  * $\hat{=}$ significant at the 5 per cent level.

63

Table 4.2 OLS-estimation results for the West German real demand for money: M1 (all logarithms)

	const.	$\left(\dfrac{M}{P}\right)_{t-1}$	$\left(\dfrac{Y}{P}\right)_t$	$\left(\dfrac{Y}{P}\right)_{t-1}$	$i_{M,t}$	$i_{M,t-1}$	$i_{b,t}$	$i_{b,t-1}$	e_t	f_t	f_{t-1}	$\bar{R}^2$	SEE	h
Seasonally unadjusted:														
1	-1.118	0.430 (9.03)	0.741 (12.51)		-0.050 (-5.84)						-0.057 (-2.61)	0.960	0.022	-1.785*
2	-1.005	0.437 (9.05)	0.710 (11.85)			-0.044 (-5.36)				-0.036 (-1.67)		0.958	0.023	-1.244
3	-1.121	0.443 (9.24)	0.726 (12.08)		-0.046 (-5.41)					-0.044 (-2.06)		0.958	0.023	-1.670*
4	-1.009	0.430 (8.86)	0.719 (12.02)			-0.046 (-5.58)					-0.041 (-1.91)	0.958	0.023	-1.284
5	-0.533	0.407 (7.59)	0.676 (10.70)					-0.099 (-4.50)		-0.020 (-0.86)		0.952	0.024	-0.395
Seasonally adjusted:														
6	0.707	0.909 (19.79)		-0.018 (-0.43)	-0.075 (-4.63)	0.035 (2.02)			-0.042 (-1.84)			0.985	0.011	1.236
7	1.375	0.845 (23.38)		-0.073 (-2.16)	-0.044 (-9.58)				-0.063 (-3.07)			0.984	0.012	2.603*
8	1.317	0.854 (23.93)	-0.067 (-2.08)		-0.045 (-9.48)				-0.061 (-3.01)			0.984	0.012	2.639*
9	1.295	0.857 (23.92)	-0.066 (-2.02)		-0.047 (-9.39)					-0.059 (-2.91)		0.984	0.012	2.715*
10	2.913	0.784 (19.48)	-0.245 (-5.68)					-0.118 (-9.25)	-0.064 (-3.10)			0.983	0.012	2.741*
11	3.038	0.771 (19.48)		-0.256 (-6.12)				-0.112 (-9.76)	-0.073 (-3.53)			0.984	0.012	2.623*

Note: t-values in parenthesis.
* $\hat{=}$ significant at the 5 per cent level.

lagged money market rate all have significant influences. In the seasonally adjusted data, the main influences are the lagged GNP, the exchange rate, the actual or lagged money market rate or the lagged long-term interest rate. The resulting estimated equations using the seasonally adjusted data lead to unsatisfactory results. For example, the introduction of different interest rates in the equations reduces the coefficient of the lagged money stock, but there is a change in the constant and no compensation in the GNP variable. Aside from this, the coefficient of the (lagged) GNP has a negative sign, which is implausible. Furthermore, the coefficient of the lagged money market rate is positive if it is included, but this compensates the large negative sign of the actual money market rate. A comparison of the coefficients of the money market rates with the long-term interest rates shows that the latter has, in absolute terms, a larger influence on the demand for money.

The discrepancies between the results are somewhat smaller using estimates for the unadjusted data. Here the GNP variables have a greater influence than the lagged money variable and the absolute value of the long-term rate is distinctly larger than that of the money market rate.

Evaluations of the different procedures show that with the seasonally adjusted data, the regressions have a higher $\bar{R}^2$ (about 0.984 as opposed to 0.958 when using the unadjusted data) and a smaller standard error (1.2 per cent and 2.3 per cent respectively). For both types of regressions, however, in many cases the hypothesis of autocorrelation cannot be rejected.

4.2.2 Regressions for the Quantity of Money M2

In general, the money stock variable M2 does not yield very good results for the specification of the demand for money in the Federal Republic of Germany (see Schlomann, 1988). Therefore, only the notable points will be discussed. A summary of the results can be found in Tables 4.3 and 4.4. Apart from the GNP variables, the lagged money variable as well as the actual and lagged long-term interest rates, there are no other significant influences. For nominal and real estimates, using unadjusted data, the resulting signs are implausible for the influences of the rate of interest, although the coefficients are significant. In the case of real estimates, using unadjusted data, the interest rate influence is in most cases insignificant. On the other hand, the coefficients for the actual as well as the lagged

66

Table 4.3 OLS-estimation results for the West German nominal demand for money: M2 (all logarithms)

	const.	M_{t-1}	Y_t	Y_{t-1}	$i_{M,t}$	$i_{M,t-1}$	$i_{b,t}$	$i_{b,t-1}$	e_t	f_t	f_{t-1}	P_t	$\bar{R}^2$	SEE	h
Seasonally unadjusted:															
1	-0.280	0.813 (12.86)	0.488 (10.17)	-0.116 (-2.03)			0.047 (1.35)	-0.019 (-0.52)		0.003 (0.14)		-0.182 (-1.48)	0.997	0.015	-0.697
2	-0.507	0.739 (14.57)	0.453 (11.89)	-0.111 (-1.95)			0.033 (2.31)						0.997	0.015	0.353
3	-0.656	0.660 (21.36)	0.443 (11.22)				0.046 (3.56)				-0.006 (-0.45)		0.997	0.015	0.411
4	-0.663	0.658 (21.64)	0.445 (11.43)				0.046 (3.60)						0.997	0.015	0.523
Seasonally adjusted:															
5	0.252	0.914 (17.04)		0.058 (1.79)				-0.028 (-2.34)			-0.020 (-1.71)		0.991	0.012	0.751
6	0.171	0.948 (18.64)		0.037 (1.21)				-0.035 (-3.06)					0.991	0.012	1.097
7	0.140	0.962 (19.07)	0.029 (0.95)					-0.036 (-3.12)					0.991	0.012	0.978

Note: t-values in parenthesis.

Table 4.4 OLS-estimation results for the West German real demand for money: M2 (all logarithms)

	const.	$\left(\frac{M}{P}\right)_{t-1}$	$\left(\frac{Y}{P}\right)_t$	$\left(\frac{Y}{P}\right)_{t-1}$	$i_{M,t}$	$i_{M,t-1}$	$i_{b,t}$	$i_{b,t-1}$	e_t	f_t	f_{t-1}	$\bar{R}^2$	SEE	h
Seasonally unadjusted:														
1	-1.198	0.822 (19.97)	0.499 (11.56)	-0.119 (-2.05)			0.029 (0.83)	-0.015 (-0.42)		0.010 (0.65)		0.987	0.015	-0.725
2	-1.206	0.821 (20.52)	0.500 (11.76)	-0.119 (-2.10)		0.014 (0.96)					0.011 (0.73)	0.987	0.015	-0.609
3	-1.155	0.829 (22.58)	0.496 (12.25)	-0.130 (-2.48)	0.015 (1.11)		0.015 (1.11)					0.988	0.015	-0.642
4	-1.262	0.815 (20.45)	0.505 (12.10)	-0.109 (-1.93)			0.018 (1.31)					0.988	0.015	-0.571
5	-1.522	0.762 (29.45)	0.492 (11.59)				0.027 (2.13)					0.987	0.015	-0.334
Seasonally unadjusted:														
6	0.144	0.944 (21.36)	0.047 (1.54)					-0.040 (-3.01)		-0.072 (-1.80)	0.060 (1.61)	0.947	0.013	0.423
7	0.134	0.944 (21.30)		0.050 (1.66)				-0.041 (-3.15)			0.056 (1.56)	0.947	0.013	0.423
8	-0.495	0.971 (29.64)		0.055 (1.97)				-0.052 (-4.65)	-0.068 (-1.74)			0.946	0.013	0.225
9	0.142	0.948 (21.00)	0.046 (1.50)					-0.046 (-3.64)	-0.013 (-0.80)			0.946	0.013	0.308
10	-0.578	0.973 (29.45)	0.055 (1.91)					-0.051 (-4.38)				0.946	0.013	0.188

Note: *t*-values in parenthesis.

GNP were significant, although the lagged GNP has a negative sign which compensates the large coefficient of the actual GNP and the lagged money stock. In this case the interest rate coefficients are, as expected, negative and significant.

The adjusted R^2 is clearly lower for the real regressions than for the nominal regressions in most cases. The standard deviations are between 1.2 per cent and 1.5 per cent. The hypothesis of no first-order autocorrelation cannot be rejected, because the absolute value of the h-statistic is less than 1.645 in all cases.

4.2.3　Regressions for the Quantity of Money M3

The estimated equations for the nominal money stock M3 (see Table 4.5) show that for the unadjusted data the significant influences are the actual money market rate or the lagged long-term interest rate, aside from the lagged money variable and the actual and lagged GNP. The exchange and forward rates as well as the price index have insignificant coefficients. With regard to the seasonally adjusted data, aside from the lagged money and the actual GNP variables, the lagged forward rate and the exchange rates are relevant influences. Noticeable is that the exchange rate has a significant value only if the lagged forward rate is also considered, although the lagged forward rate remains insignificant. This is a clear sign of the high correlation between these two variables.

For the quantity of money M3, it is also clear that the influence of the long-term interest rates is considerably stronger than that of the money market rate. The negative coefficient of the exchange rate is subject to large deviations, according to whether the implicit (although implausible opposite) influence of the lagged forward rate is considered.

The estimates are good. The adjusted R^2 is over 0.996 and the standard error is under 1 per cent. The h-statistic indicates autocorrelation in only two cases for the unadjusted data.

The results for the real money stock M3 are similar to those for the nominal money stock M3. Besides the lagged money variable and the actual GNP, the equation using the unadjusted data has significant coefficients for the lagged GNP along with the money market rate. Using the seasonally adjusted data, neither the actual nor the lagged GNP have a significant influence. Instead, the lagged long-term rate as well as the exchange rate and the lagged forward rate show significant results. The relation between the exchange and forward

Table 4.5 OLS-estimation results for the West German nominal demand for money: M3 (all logarithms)

	const.	M_{t-1}	Y_t	Y_{t-1}	$i_{M,t}$	$i_{M,t-1}$	$i_{b,t}$	$i_{b,t-1}$	e_t	f_t	f_{t-1}	P_{t-1}	R^2	SEE	h
Seasonally unadjusted:															
1	-0.217	0.598	0.236	0.111				-0.027	-0.023			0.193	0.999	0.009	0.699
		(9.35)	(8.43)	(3.41)				(-3.44)	(-1.56)			(1.89)			
2	-0.800	0.697	0.254	0.105				-0.021					0.999	0.009	0.680
		(18.91)	(9.54)	(3.20)				(-3.03)							
3	-0.125	0.709	0.260	0.106	-0.010							-0.022	0.999	0.009	0.463
		(15.57)	(9.50)	(3.19)	(-3.00)							(-0.43)			
4	-0.144	0.698	0.258	0.107	-0.010								0.999	0.009	0.529
		(18.96)	(9.65)	(3.26)	(-3.03)										
Seasonally adjusted:															
5	0.812	0.813	-0.158	0.240			-0.004	-0.044		-0.013		0.011	0.997	0.007	1.877*
		(8.06)	(-1.30)	(2.25)			(-0.23)	(-2.15)		(-1.01)		(0.12)			
6	0.888	0.783		0.108				-0.043	-0.053		0.039		0.997	0.007	1.305
		(10.42)		(2.70)				(-6.02)	(-2.58)		(1.92)				
7	1.002	0.755		0.123				-0.048	-0.019				0.996	0.007	1.702*
		(9.97)		(3.02)				(-7.13)	(-1.71)						
8	0.712	0.829	0.084					-0.040	-0.052		0.043		0.996	0.007	0.966
		(9.87)	(1.85)					(-5.50)	(-2.36)		(2.07)				
9	0.824	0.802	0.098					-0.045	-0.014				0.996	0.008	1.351
		(9.36)	(2.11)					(-6.54)	(-1.12)						

Note: t-values in parenthesis.
* $\hat{=}$ significant at the 5 per cent level.

Table 4.6 OLS-estimation results for the West German real demand for money: M3 (all logarithms)

const.	$\left(\frac{M}{P}\right)_{t-1}$	$\left(\frac{Y}{P}\right)_t$	$\left(\frac{Y}{P}\right)_{t-1}$	$i_{M,t}$	$i_{M,t-1}$	$i_{b,t}$	$i_{b,t-1}$	e_t	f_t	f_{t-1}	R^2	SEE	h
Seasonally unadjusted:													
1 −0.806	0.789 (25.49)	0.277 (9.14)	0.098 (2.76)	−0.016 (−4.50)					0.015 (1.15)		0.994	0.010	0.486
2 −0.508	0.800 (22.99)	0.253 (7.63)	0.066 (1.76)				−0.028 (−3.10)				0.993	0.011	1.844*
3 −0.721	0.802 (26.37)	0.266 (8.86)	0.082 (2.37)	−0.016 (−4.50)							0.994	0.010	0.784
4 −0.806	0.789 (25.43)	0.277 (9.14)	0.098 (2.76)	−0.016 (−4.51)				0.015 (1.62)			0.994	0.010	0.486
5 −0.570	0.853 (39.50)	0.264 (8.26)		−0.015 (−4.07)				0.008 (0.82)			0.993	0.010	0.295
Seasonally adjusted:													
6 1.186	0.883 (18.44)	−0.051 (−1.76)				0.020 (0.72)	−0.077 (−2.68)	−0.103 (−2.90)		0.093 (2.98)	0.976	0.009	0.854
7 1.045	0.899 (21.11)	−0.045 (−1.63)					−0.057 (−6.51)	−0.087 (−3.12)		0.080 (3.20)	0.976	0.009	0.842
8 1.027	0.900 (20.95)		−0.043 (−1.58)				−0.056 (−6.65)	−0.087 (−3.10)		0.079 (3.17)	0.976	0.009	0.805
9 1.147	0.893 (19.23)	−0.052 (−1.73)					−0.066 (−7.30)	−0.012 (−0.74)			0.974	0.010	1.779*

Note: t-values in parenthesis.
* $\hat{=}$ significant at the 5 per cent level.

rate, as described above, is also valid for the last two variables in this case.

The adjusted R^2 is 0.994 for the unadjusted data and 0.976 for the seasonally adjusted data. The standard error is around 1 per cent in both cases and there is little indication of autocorrelation.

4.3 THE STABILITY OF THE REGRESSIONS

The above results show several successful estimates for the different definitions of the money stock in the Federal Republic of Germany. However, the crucial evidence is whether the estimated coefficients have remained stable during the observation period. With a structural break within this time period, monetary policy would have been dangerously based on a functional relationship which is no longer valid. To clarify this essential point the entire period (1974–87) has been divided into two subperiods, that is from 1974–80 and from 1981 to the beginning of 1987. Different functions are then estimated for these subperiods. The 1974–87 period has been further divided into three shorter subperiods – 1974–78, 1979–82 and 1983–87 (first quarter). As the results from the second subdivision support the evidence obtained previously for the two longer subperiods, we do not illustrate their results in a detailed manner. Although the regressions considered here do in some instances yield insignificant coefficients for the entire period (1974–87), more significant coefficients could be obtained for the two subperiods 1974–80 and 1981–87 whenever there was evidence of a structural break (see also Schlomann, 1988). The econometric results are presented in Tables 4.7 to 4.10.

It is evident that for the period between 1974 and 1980, all of the estimates with unadjusted data have significant coefficients, but the hypothesis of autocorrelation cannot be rejected for two of the M1 estimates. For the estimates using seasonally adjusted data, every equation, except one M1 equation, has at least one parameter which remains insignificant at the 5 per cent level. Therefore, the coefficients for the exchange rate and lagged forward rate in the M3 equations are most affected, but the actual and the lagged GNP, too, no longer have a statistically significant influence in many cases. Especially with the seasonally adjusted data, the hypothesis of autocorrelation can be rejected for all of the analysed functions.

For the time period from 1980 to 1987 the picture is completely different. For the parameters estimated from the unadjusted data,

Table 4.7 OLS-estimation results for the West German nominal demand for money from 1974 to 1980 (all logarithms)

	const.	M_{t-1}	Y_t	Y_{t-1}	$i_{M,t}$	$i_{M,t-1}$	$i_{b,t}$	$i_{b,t-1}$	e_t	f_t	f_{t-1}	P_t	$\bar{R}^2$	SEE	h
Seasonally unadjusted:															
M1	-0.780	0.123 (1.86)	0.574 (11.38)			-0.071 (-10.40)				-0.222 (-5.26)		0.537 (3.65)	0.997	0.010	1.130
M1	-0.254	0.281 (5.93)	0.753 (16.74)								-0.174 (-4.06)		0.997	0.011	-1.913*
M3	0.068	0.597 (10.49)	0.323 (8.65)	0.129 (2.68)	-0.070 (-9.36)			-0.044 (-3.90)					0.998	0.009	-0.222
M3	-0.167	0.640 (10.79)	0.320 (7.79)	0.114 (2.18)	-0.014 (-2.95)								0.997	0.009	0.502
Seasonally adjusted:															
M1	1.095	0.683 (8.23)		0.131 (2.36)	-0.038 (-5.71)					-0.085 (-2.37)			0.994	0.009	0.589
M1	1.126	0.688 (7.17)	0.121 (1.89)		-0.037 (-5.26)					-0.091 (-2.43)			0.993	0.009	0.276
M3	0.427	0.875 (7.77)		0.078 (1.58)			-0.041 (-3.76)		-0.021 (-0.51)		-0.051 (-1.39)		0.995	0.007	0.659
M3	0.317	0.909 (7.22)	0.058 (1.03)				-0.039 (-3.51)		-0.021 (-0.46)		-0.052 (-1.38)		0.994	0.007	0.426

Note: t-values in parenthesis.

* $\hat{=}$ significant at the 5 per cent level.

Table 4.8 OLS-estimation results for the West German real demand for money from 1974 to 1980 (all logarithms)

	const.	$\left(\frac{M}{P}\right)_{t-1}$	$\left(\frac{Y}{P}\right)_t$	$\left(\frac{Y}{P}\right)_{t-1}$	$i_{M,t}$	$i_{M,t-1}$	$i_{b,t}$	$i_{b,t-1}$	e_t	f_t	f_{t-1}	R^2	SEE	h
Seasonally unadjusted:														
M1	0.453	0.260 (3.86)	0.655 (11.75)			-0.070 (-8.30)					-0.209 (-4.22)	0.988	0.013	-0.510
M1	-0.306	0.285 (5.05)	0.759 (15.26)		-0.073 (-9.78)						-0.187 (-4.50)	0.990	0.011	-1.941*
M3	-0.757	0.662 (12.77)	0.368 (8.67)	0.142 (2.73)	-0.021 (-4.51)							0.991	0.009	0
Seasonally adjusted:														
M1	0.263	0.889 (9.18)		0.067 (0.50)	-0.057 (-2.38)	-0.027 (-1.12)			-0.008 (-0.13)			0.937	0.011	0.770
M1	2.723	0.777 (10.51)		-0.221 (-2.27)				-0.081 (-5.79)	-0.058 (-1.33)			0.946	0.010	0.546
M3	0.117	0.898 (14.66)		0.103 (1.18)				-0.052 (-5.30)	-0.017 (-0.36)		0.087 (2.14)	0.934	0.008	0.559
M3	0.379	0.895 (14.33)	0.063 (0.73)					-0.051 (-4.62)	-0.030 (-0.65)		0.082 (1.96)	0.931	0.009	0.449

Note: *t*-values in parenthesis.
* $\hat{=}$ significant at the 5 per cent level.

Table 4.9 OLS-estimation results for the West German nominal demand for money from 1981 to 1987, first quarter (all logarithms)

	const.	M_{t-1}	Y_t	Y_{t-1}	$i_{M,t}$	$i_{M,t-1}$	$i_{b,t}$	$i_{b,t-1}$	e_t	f_t	f_{t-1}	P_t	$\bar{R}^2$	SEE	h
Seasonally unadjusted:															
M1	0.359	0.143 (0.99)	0.566 (4.35)			-0.093 (-2.06)				-0.077 (-1.21)		0.270 (0.59)	0.938	0.027	-1.735*
M1	0.763	0.222 (1.86)	0.634 (6.32)		-0.092 (-2.36)						-0.061 (-1.33)		0.939	0.027	-1.994*
M3	0.075	0.713 (10.58)	0.203 (6.23)	0.113 (2.93)				-0.022 (-0.93)					0.995	0.007	0.956
M3	0.038	0.714 (11.26)	0.201 (6.25)	0.116 (2.99)	-0.012 (-1.03)								0.995	0.007	0.949
Seasonally adjusted:															
M1	1.015	0.695 (12.18)		0.135 (2.41)	-0.051 (-5.45)					-0.067 (-4.93)			0.991	0.007	-0.365
M1	0.958	0.673 (12.01)	0.164 (2.92)		-0.048 (-5.16)					-0.071 (-5.36)			0.992	0.007	0.469
M3	1.251	0.590 (4.54)		0.264 (2.76)				-0.039 (-1.98)	-0.047 (-1.74)		-0.018 (-0.53)		0.991	0.006	-1.217
M3	1.245	0.622 (3.65)	0.231 (1.81)					-0.042 (-1.97)	-0.053 (-1.79)		-0.010 (-0.23)		0.989	0.007	-1.767*

Note: t-values in parenthesis.
* $\hat{=}$ significant at the 5 per cent level.

Table 4.10 OLS-estimation results for the West German real demand for money from 1981 to 1987, first quarter (all logarithms)

const.	$\left(\frac{M}{P}\right)_{t-1}$	$\left(\frac{Y}{P}\right)_t$	$\left(\frac{Y}{P}\right)_{t-1}$	$i_{M,t}$	$i_{M,t-1}$	$i_{b,t}$	$i_{b,t-1}$	e_t	f_t	f_{t-1}	$\bar{R}^2$	SEE	h
Seasonally unadjusted:													
M1 1.268	0.165 (1.24)	0.600 (5.44)			-0.093 (-3.13)					-0.074 (-1.52)	0.861	0.027	1.574
M1 0.895	0.212 (1.67)	0.617 (5.59)		-0.083 (-2.98)						-0.079 (-1.54)	0.857	0.027	-2.071*
M3 -0.216	0.741 (10.75)	0.221 (6.33)	0.114 (2.75)	-0.024 (-3.17)							0.986	0.008	0.586
Seasonally adjusted:													
M1 1.425	0.662 (6.90)		0.095 (1.11)	-0.028 (-0.92)	-0.019 (-0.66)			-0.099 (-3.90)			0.972	0.009	0.741
M1 2.506	0.592 (11.52)		-0.002 (-0.00)				-0.106 (-6.22)	-0.105 (-6.07)			0.976	0.008	0.362
M3 1.808	0.533 (4.28)		0.234 (2.09)				-0.040 (-2.39)	-0.066 (-2.14)		-0.034 (-0.81)	0.971	0.007	-1.246
M3 1.750	0.514 (4.33)	0.262 (2.44)					-0.031 (-1.66)	-0.058 (-1.88)		-0.049 (-1.14)	0.973	0.007	-1.149

Note: *t*-values in parenthesis.
* $\hat{=}$ significant at the 5 per cent level.

the coefficients for the exchange rate and the forward rate lose their significance. This is also true for the lagged demand for money in the M1 regressions as well as the interest rate in the M3 regressions. Also, the hypothesis of autocorrelation can no longer be rejected in nearly all the equations for M1. With the regressions estimated from the seasonally adjusted data, the nominal M1 functions still have significant estimated coefficients, but the other estimates produce coefficients which are insignificant in most cases. This is primarily the case for the exchange and forward rates (with the exception of the real M1 functions) and occasionally for the GNP variable (but in most of the functions, the GNP variable has a higher level of significance than for the period from 1974 to 1980). For one of these functions the hypothesis of autocorrelation cannot be rejected for the period between 1980 and 1987.

It is notable that the importance of the forward rate is diminished in the second sub-period for the M1 specifications and it becomes insignificant. This means that during this time period, the importance of external economic influences was reduced. The reason for this can be that the external factors are relevant mainly in a phase where the Deutsche Mark is devalued. That was before 1980 (as well as after 1985), when there was a stronger foreign demand for Deutsche Marks (see also Schlomann, 1988).

The estimates of the coefficients which are sometimes distinctly different from each other in the different time periods, suggest a possible structural break at the end of 1980. To investigate this possibility, Chow-tests are performed for the different functions whose estimated parameters for both sub-periods are somewhat significant. The results are shown in Table 4.11. They indicate no structural break at the end of 1980 for all estimates based on the nominal quantity of money. On the other hand, the test statistics indicate distinctly higher values for the real equations. For the M1 specification using seasonally adjusted data, a structural break is indicated using a 5 per cent level. For the tested M3 regression, using unadjusted data, the hypothesis of a structural break is only barely rejected at the 5 per cent level.

These results should be viewed with caution because the test assumes a constant variance for the different time periods. This is not always the case. On the other hand, other tests of instability also use very restrictive assumptions.

In general, the Chow-tests show that for most of the functions there is no structural break at the end of 1980. However, the

Table 4.11   Results of the Chow-test for alternative estimates for
West Germany: 1980 (4th quarter)

Endogenous Variable (All logarithms)	Exogenous Variables	Empirical F
Seasonally unadjusted:		
$M1_t$	$M1_{t-1}$, Y_t, $i_{M,t}$, f_{t-1}	1.78
	(Table 4.1)	
$M3_t$	$M3_{t-1}$, Y_t, Y_{t-1}, $i_{M,t}$	1.41
	(Table 4.5)	
$\left(\frac{M1}{P}\right)_t$	$\left(\frac{M1}{P}\right)_{t-1}$, $\left(\frac{Y}{P}\right)_t$, $i_{M,t-1}$, f_{t-1}	2.97
	(Table 4.2)	
$\left(\frac{M1}{P}\right)_t$	$\left(\frac{M1}{P}\right)_{t-1}$, $\left(\frac{Y}{P}\right)_t$, $i_{M,t}$, f_{t-1}	2.80
	(Table 4.2)	
$\left(\frac{M3}{P}\right)_t$	$\left(\frac{M3}{P}\right)_{t-1}$, $\left(\frac{Y}{P}\right)_t$, $\left(\frac{Y}{P}\right)_{t-1}$, $i_{M,t}$	3.92
	(Table 4.6)	
Seasonally adjusted:		
$M1_t$	$M1_{t-1}$, Y_{t-1}, $i_{M,t}$, f_t	1.54
	(Table 4.1)	
$M1_t$	$M1_{t-1}$, Y_t, $i_{M,t}$, f_t	1.61
	(Table 4.1)	
$\left(\frac{M1}{P}\right)_t$	$\left(\frac{M1}{P}\right)_{t-1}$, $\left(\frac{Y}{P}\right)_{t-1}$, $i_{b,t-1}$, e_t	7.00*
	(Table 4.2)	

Note: * $\triangleq$ significant at 5 per cent level.

regressions for the period between 1981 and 1987 show that the
opportunity cost variables do not have significant estimates of the
parameters. The relatively good results of the Chow-tests should not
conceal the fact that the demand for money in the 1980s has become
considerably more uncertain, not only because of the existence of
abrupt breaks in otherwise stable estimated functions, but also because the variance of the estimated coefficients has greatly increased.

These observations are based on time periods which are characterised firstly by the consequences of the second oil price shock of 1979
(high balance of payments deficits, a weak US$ compared to the
Deutsche Mark, relatively high rates of inflation), and secondly by an
intensified introduction of financial innovations in money markets
and a further internationalisation of the whole spectrum of money
and bond markets around the world.

4.4   SUMMARY

At first, several functions seem to describe the different forms of the
demand for money in the Federal Republic of Germany quite satisfactorily. This judgement has to be reconsidered after studying the
regressions for the sub-periods from 1974 to 1980 and from 1980 to
1987, the reason being that, especially in the second sub-period,
estimates for the parameters of the opportunity cost variables became insignificant. The most acceptable function remains Equation 7
in Table 4.1, where the nominal money stock M1, computed on the
basis of seasonally adjusted data, is dependent on the lagged money
stock, lagged GNP, the money market interest rate and the forward
rate. Also acceptable is Equation 3 in Table 4.6, where the real
money stock M3, computed on the basis of unadjusted data, is
dependent on the lagged money variable, the actual and lagged GNP
and the money market rate.

Finally, it is clear that the estimates of the demand for money in
the 1980s are associated with more uncertainty than in the 1970s. It
seems likely that the explanation lies not only in a structural break,
but also in the fact that the influence of several variables, in particular
the opportunity cost variables, fluctuates strongly with time. That is
confirmed by estimates for the period between 1983 and 1987, where
the estimates for the opportunity cost variables also lack significance.
This phenomenon brings considerable uncertainty as to the effects of
monetary policy measures, which are after all oriented to stabilising
the growth of the money stock and with it the demand for money.
One possible explanation may be the growing interdependence of
international money markets as well as the continuous flow of financial
innovations, which have created increasing difficulties generally for
central bank control and the supervision of financial markets.

The post-1987 demand for money in Germany has been further
influenced by other special factors, such as the increased holding of

DM notes abroad and, in the second half of 1988, a preference for cash on the part of German investors following the introduction of a withholding tax on capital income scheduled for the beginning of 1989. More important has been – from the middle of 1990 onwards – the expected destabilising effect on the German demand for money of the political and economic changes in East Germany and the unification of the two Germanies. In the past, the Deutsche Mark had in fact been used as a parallel currency in the territory of the former German Democratic Republic, but the share of the Deutsche Mark as a percentage of the total money in circulation in East Germany remained small and was fairly constant over time. However, since the breakdown of the East German political system in November 1989, the demand for the Deutsche Mark by the East German population increased substantially until a currency union between East and West Germany taking effect from July 1990 replaced the East German by the Deutsche Mark.

In the likely event of the demand for money in East Germany depending on variables other than in West Germany, or of their being determined in a different fashion, there would be bound to develop a structural break and/or a period of instability in the overall demand-for-money function in Germany. The indications are that the velocity of circulation will be lower in East Germany (after a possible initial rise) than in West Germany as – at least until German reunification was mooted – East Germany showed no signs of the type of financial innovations which in Western Europe and the United States have played such a dominant role since the early 1970s; the influence of the opportunity cost variables cannot therefore be expected to be very strong for some time. (In the GDR asset holding of residents was restricted to cash, demand deposits and saving deposits.) Because there were no competing financial markets, interest rates could be fixed by the government and did not differ between those set by the Staatsbank (central bank) of the GDR and other state-owned banks, and moved very little over time. From 1971 onwards, the rate of interest on all demand and saving deposits remained unchanged at 3.25 per cent.

There is no doubt that East German residents will soon acquaint themselves with portfolio management and financial innovations which the currency union and increasing competition will bring about – not least under the influence of West German and foreign financial institutions now moving into the East German market. Thus the influence of the opportunity cost variables is likely to become stronger in time and it may well become more difficult for the German monetary authorities to control and supervise their financial markets. Another factor to reckon with will be the international strength of the Deutsche Mark which ultimately will depend on economic growth, the balance of payments position and the economic and political stability in the unified Germany. Of these factors, the influence of the external ones will be of particular relevance as far as a possible appreciation of the Deutsche Mark is concerned, and this latter factor again will be determined by the economic situation in the unified Germany and expectations regarding its future economic trends.

Notes

* The authors are grateful to Philip Arestis, Herbert Buscher and Victoria Chick for their comments and also wish to thank the Economics Department of the Deutsche Bundesbank for kindly supplying essential data.

1. For subsequent findings of an unstable West German demand for money during the mid and late 1980s, see Buscher and Frowen (1990).
2. The authors are fully aware of recent developments in British applied econometrics as exemplified in Buscher and Frowen (1990). This paper, however, attempts to discuss the demand for money within the traditional German approach.
3. For an application of this model to the demand for money in small developing economies, see Arestis (1988).

References

Arestis, P. (1988) 'The Demand for Money in Small Developing Economies: An Application of the Error Correction Mechanism', in P. Arestis (ed) *Contemporary Issues in Money and Banking. Essays in Honour of Stephen Frowen* (London: Macmillan; New York: St. Martin's Press).

Buscher, H. S. (1984a) 'Zur Stabilität der Geldnachfrage. Eine empirische Betrachtung', *Kredit und Kapital*, 17, pp. 507–39.

Buscher, H. S. (1984b) 'The Stability of the West German Demand for Money, 1965–1982', *Weltwirtschaftliches Archiv*, 120, pp. 256–78.

Buscher, H. S. and Frowen, S. F. (1990) 'The Stability of the Demand for Money in the US, the UK, France, Japan and West Germany, 1973 to 1988', University College London *Discussion Papers in Economics*, No. 90–05. Also published in S. F. Frowen (ed.) *Monetary Theory and Monetary Policy: New Tracks for the 1990s* (London: Macmillan, 1992).

Buscher, H. S. and Schroeder W. (1983) 'Instabilität der Geldhaltung stellt Geldmengenziel in Frage', *Wirtschaftsdienst*, 63, pp. 309–12.
Neumann, M. J. M. (1983): 'Stabilität der Geldnachfrage und Geldpolitik', *Wirtschaftsdienst*, 63, pp. 415–20.
Schlomann, H. (1988): 'Zur Spezifikation einer Geldnachfragefunktion für die Bundesrepublik Deutschland von 1974 bis 1986', *IFO-Studien*, 34, no. 1, pp. 43–68.

5 The Effects of Financial Innovation and Deregulation on French Monetary Policy*

Robert Raymond

Through innovation and deregulation, the French financial system is presently undergoing extensive changes. It will have far-reaching implications for monetary policy.

I NEW WAYS OF FINANCING THE ECONOMY

Until the beginning of the 1980s, the financing of the French economy rested on bank intermediation, while the securities markets played only a limited role. Since 1980 these markets have strongly developed and they now occupy a central position. A brief review of the causes of this development will be followed by a description of the present structure of the financial system.

5.1 THE CAUSES OF THE BOOM IN MARKETABLE SECURITIES

To take only the fundamental causes, the following should be mentioned:

1. the marked shift in the structure of sectoral financial surpluses and deficits;
2. the active involvement of the authorities.

Table 5.1 The shifting structure of French sectoral financial surpluses and deficits, 1979–1988

	1979	1980	1981	1982	1983	1984	1985	1986	1987	1988
Companies	−3.4	−5.0	−4.2	−4.4	−2.7	−2.0	−1.9	−0.9	−1.4	−1.8
General government	−0.8	0	−1.9	−2.8	−3.2	−2.8	−2.9	−2.7	−2.0	−1.4
Households	+4.2	+3.6	+4.9	+4.6	+3.9	+3.5	+3.4	+2.6	+1.5	+1.7

5.1.1 The Shift in the Structure of French Sectoral Financial Surpluses and Deficits

The borrowing requirement of the corporate sector, which stood at close to 5 per cent of GDP at the beginning of the 1980s, declined steadily until 1986 (Table 5.1). Afterwards, the substantial investment drive, which was made possible thanks to the continuing improvement in the corporate financial situation, led to a slight increase in the borrowing requirement. Conversely, the borrowing requirement of general government (central and local government and social security funds) has risen from a very low level to around 3 per cent of GDP. However, this rate was halved between 1985 and 1988 because of attempts at stabilising the budget deficit and of higher tax receipts stemming from a strong economic activity.

The financial surplus of the household sector has shown a decline. This has been first at the expense of a sharp fall in housing investment. Then the household sector has shown an increased preference for financial market paper over traditional bank deposits. There has been a sharp widening of the differential between the net return on market investments and that on bank deposits bearing regulated rates of interest, due both to the spontaneous development of market rates and to the tax regime.

The developments led to a decline in bank intermediation in favour of financial market intermediation between 1983 and 1986. This intermediation ratio has been on a slightly upward trend since then.

5.1.2 The Active Involvement of the Authorities

The active role played by the authorities in the process of financial innovation and modernisation of the financing of the economy is without doubt one of the most striking features of the experience in France.

This role undoubtedly sprang from the need to improve government debt management techniques (creation of markets in short-term negotiable securities) or to reduce budget expenditure (reduction in the proportion of credit granted at preferential rates).

It was, however, also the authorities' aim to strengthen competition so as to bring about a better allocation of resources and reduce the cost of intermediation.

Finally, the creation of a unified capital market was an essential first step towards implementing a more active interest rate policy and abandoning an increasingly fossilised system of rigid credit restrictions.

5.2   RECENT DEVELOPMENTS ON THE FINANCIAL MARKETS

The traditional markets (stocks and shares) have seen a substantial expansion in activity. The foundations for markets in short-term negotiable securities and financial futures were laid in 1985. The virtually uninterrupted rise since 1979 in the share of markets financing the economy continued until 1986. Then, a moderate decline was noted but the October 1987 stock market crash would certainly have involved a stronger decrease in market financing without the hedging opportunities offered by the MATIF and the possibility to shift from the long end to the short end of the market.

5.2.1   The Equity Market

On the equity market, gross public issues by listed companies rose from FRF 3 billion in 1979 to FRF 58.7 billion in 1989 while the market value increased from FRF 234.8 billion to FRF 1952 billion and the volume of transactions from FRF 48.1 to FRF 668 billion.

Apart from this structural development, the expansion of the market has been encouraged on the supply side by a series of measures designed to stimulate issuing activity and new listings and on the demand side by tax measures and the favourable development of share prices (linked to the recovery of corporate profitability).

The Stimulation of Supply of Equities

The objective of the reforms was to facilitate access to the market by companies to which it was closed either because of their size or because of the structure of their share ownership.

1. In order to promote the issue of equity-equivalent securities by family firms or nationalised companies, types of non-voting shares were introduced: *'actions à dividende prioritaire'* (preferred stocks), *'certificats d'investissement'* (preference shares with fixed rate of return and profit element).
2. In order to facilitate access to the stock market by medium-sized firms, a 'second market' was created, in between the official and over-the-counter markets. This reform was inspired by foreign experience (the Unlisted Securities Market in the United Kingdom). The criteria for admission to the second market are less restrictive than those of the official market.

Measures were also taken to encourage firms to strengthen their capital base: the registration fee on cash increases in capital was abolished; since 1983 firms have been able to offer their shareholders shares in payment of dividend, and so on.

The Boom in Demand for Equities

The so-called 'Monory' Law of 13 July 1978, replaced by a new scheme, namely savings accounts composed of shares (*compte d'épargne en actions*) aimed at giving fresh impetus to personal shareholding by enabling net investment in French shares to be deducted from taxable income (up to a ceiling of FRF 5000 per married couple). This objective was indeed attained, since in 1981 1.5 million taxpaying households took advantage of the tax exemption, while share ownership rose to 10 per cent of households compared with 5 per cent in 1975. Nonetheless, the decisive factor in the renewed demand for securities has, without any doubt, been the substantial increase in share prices since 1983.

5.2.2 The Bond Market

Issue volume

Long a marginal source of financing, the bond market has grown considerably. As shown in the Table 5.2, the volume of gross issues increased sharply from 1980 onwards, reaching 5.4 per cent of GDP in 1989, compared with 5.9 per cent in 1988. Transactions on the secondary market rose from FRF 63.2 billion in 1980 to FRF 3309

Table 5.2   Gross issues in the French bond market, 1972–89

	1972	1979	1980	1985	1986	1987	1988	1989
In billions of French francs	28.9	65.6	111.7	310	345	285	333	327
As a percentage of GDP	2.9	2.7	4.0	6.6	6.8	5.4	5.9	5.4

Table 5.3   Net bond issues/GDP in West Germany, UK, France, USA and Japan in 1985 and 1988 (%)

	1985	1988
West Germany	4.3	1.9
United Kingdom	3.0	0.5
France	5.2	4.0
United States	13.8	11.3
Japan	7.7	7.4

billion in 1989. The market value of bonds trebled over the same period (from FRF 567.4 billion at end 1980 to FRF 2211 billion at end 1989.)

Measured by the ratio of net issues to GDP, the French bond primary market is the largest in Europe (Table 5.3).

Share in the Financing of the Economy

Directly or indirectly (issues by financial institutions), net bond issues accounted for over half of the change in non-financial sectors' domestic debt (total domestic credit) in 1985, compared with less than 20 per cent, in 1975. This proportion declined more recently to 12 per cent in 1989, because of various factors: a change in expectations about interest rates, the extent of the sale of shares by the state (privatisation programme) and above all, the increased reliance of firms on bank credit to finance their liquidity needs.

The Issuers

The marked increase in the budget deficit from 1980 onwards and the desire to keep money creation by the Treasury within strict limits caused the government to turn to the bond market. A prudential concern to consolidate their funding and the highly restrictive control of bank lending financed by monetary resources were a strong incentive for the financial institutions to increase their issuing activity.

Table 5.4   Distribution of gross bond issues in France, 1975–89

	1975	1980	1985	1989
Central government		27.7	30.2	28.8
Other general government	11.7	5.3	4.9	0.4
Banks	25.1	33.2	38.6	20.7
Other financial institutions	36.1	19.8	16.0	34.7
Non-financial companies	28.6	13.0	8.5	13.5
Non-residents	0.5	1.0	1.8	1.9
	100.0	100.0	100.0	100.0

More recently the latter strengthened their capital ratio in order to comply with the requirements of the Basle agreement (Cooke ratio). They issued close substitutes for shares.

The government and bank offerings accounted for the bulk of the growth in the primary bond market. The share of non-financial companies in total issues, despite increased issuing activity by the *Grandes Entreprises Nationales*, contracted to less than 14 per cent in 1989, compared with almost 30 per cent in 1975 (Table 5.4). The number of foreign issuers remains very small, though the volume of issues increased to FRF 6.1 billion in 1989 from FRF 1.1 to 1.5 billion in the preceding years.

In the last few years the government has followed an unwritten rule limiting its share of the market to around one-third of gross issues.

An international comparison of the share in the financing of the economy through bond issues for the United States, Japan, the Federal Republic of Germany, the United Kingdom and France is given in Table 5.5.

The Investors

Three factors combined to make investment in bonds particularly attractive: high real interest rates, the steady decline in nominal rates from mid-1981 onwards and the favourable tax treatment.

Whereas from 1975 to 1980 the interest rates offered on the bond market were only slightly higher than the rate of inflation, and even on occasion lower, as in 1975 and 1979, they rose considerably during the second part of the period; since 1982 they have consistently exceeded the increase in retail prices by more than 4 points (5.3 points in 1989).

Table 5.5   Net bond issues in France in 1984 and 1988 (as a percentage of the total)

	United States		Japan		West Germany		United Kingdom		France	
	1984	1988	1984	1988	1984	1988	1984	1988	1984	1988
General government[1]	85	67	48	17	49	114	88	–	46	31
Financial institutions	5	13	35	55	49	–22	1	23	42	57
Non-financial companies	10	20	17	28	2	8	3	60	11	10
Non-residents	–	–	–	–	–[2]	–	8	17	1	2
	100	100	100	100	100	100	100	100	100	100

Note: 1. Central government, local government, administrative agencies.
   2. All the foreign issues in DM are considered as international issues.

Source: OECD, Financial Monthly Statistics, January 1989.

The tax regime also acted as a stimulus, in particular for private individuals. Income from non-indexed French bonds is subject to a withholding tax in settlement of income tax at a rate of 25 per cent (2 per cent higher since 1987 as a result of the contribution to solidarity).

Capital gains realised through the sale of securities are taxed at a rate of only 15 per cent (2 per cent higher since 1987) on amounts exceeding a tax-free allowance (FRF 298,000 in 1989). This tax advantage was all the more significant given the large capital gains that could be made as a result of the fall in interest rates as from 1982.

While the demand for securities was boosted by the improved return on bond investment, it was clearly also stimulated by the establishment of the short-term investment funds.

Two types of measures exerted a decisive influence in this direction; the tightening of ceilings on the rate of interest payable on deposit accounts and cash certificates in September 1981 and the progressive increase in tax on these instruments.

Finally, the short-term mutual funds (*fonds communs de placement* – FCPs) and short-term open-ended unit trusts (*sociétés d'investissement à capital variable* – SICAVs), which were established in 1982 in response to the tighter regulation of deposit rates, redirected savings towards the bond market. In a better position than individuals or companies to manage interest rate risks (floating rate notes, repurchase/resale options, financial futures operations), and offering investors both a very high degree of liquidity and market rates of return, these entities have been highly successful.

5.2.3 The reform of the mortgage market

Hitherto banks granting mortgage loans have refinanced this lending on the money, bond and mortgage markets, the last of which has remained relatively narrow. In future they will also be able to obtain funding from the Mortgage Refinancing Bank (*Caisse de Refinancement Hypothécaire*). Based on the American system of the Federal National Mortgage Association, the Bank raises funds by issuing long-term bonds quoted on the stock exchange and guaranteed by the government.

5.2.4 The short-term negotiable securities markets

The expansion of the transferable securities markets was achieved by refining techniques and diversifying instruments. In the process the validity of the distinctions traditionally made between financial assets was undermined:

1. the boundary between equities and bonds became blurred with the appearance of non-voting shares and subordinated loans;
2. the boundary between bonds and monetary assets became less clear due to the very high degree of liquidity of SICAV shares and the instruments which reduce the risks involved in interest rate fluctuations (bond purchases with option of resale, securities with variable or reviewable rates), which, through the short-term investment funds, have been taken up in great numbers by investors.

It therefore seemed necessary to complete the existing range of products by creating short-term negotiable securities (see Table 5.6) in order to:

1. give borrowers the choice between bank credit in all its forms, and issues of securities over virtually the full maturity range;
2. offer lenders the option between bank deposits and securities purchases across all maturities (and no longer equities and bonds alone) either directly or via SICAV and FCP.

Short-term securities have now the same characteristics as for their maturities (from 10 days to 7 years), their minimum denomination (FRF 1 million) and the interest they bear (fixed interest rate for paper at less than one year; reviewable rate possible for securities at more than 1 year).

Table 5.6 Main features of French money market securities (negotiable on markets open to all economic agents)

	Certificates of deposit	Commercial paper	Treasury Bills	Bills issued by specialised financial institutions (IFS)	Bills issued by finance companies and "Article 99" institutions
Regulation as on 1st March 1987					
Date of introduction	March 1985	December 1985	December 1985	December 1985	May 1986–March 1987
Issuers	Credit institutions which: – may accept deposits from the public at less than 2 years (banks, savings banks, municipal credit banks and CDC) – must maintain reserves against their current liabilities	Business entities (other than credit institutions) which have been in existence for more than 2 years ● companies limited by shares ● public sector firms, agricultural co-operative societies, Groupement d'intérêt économique GIE (consortium)	Treasury	● Crédit d'Equipement des Petites et Moyennes Entreprises, Comptoir des entrepreneurs, Crédit national, Crédit foncier, SDR, ... ● Bills at less than 2 years: specialised financial institutions subject to reserve requirements	Finance companies subject to reserve requirements and securities houses (article 99 of the Banking Act of 24th January 1984) (maisons de titres)

Minimum/maximum maturities	10 days to 7 years	10 days to 7 years	in practice 13 weeks to 5 years	10 days to 7 years	10 days to 7 years
Minimum denomination	FRF 1 million	FRF 1 million	FRF 1 million	FRF 1 million	FRF 1 million
Interest rates	Fixed rate / Reviewable rate (2)	Fixed rate for paper with a maturity of less than 2 years	Fixed rate	Same as FRF-denominated certificates of deposit (2)	
Reserve requirements on current liabilities	Yes, on the gross outstanding amount of certificates at less than 2 years	No	No	Yes, on the gross outstanding amount of certificates at less than 2 years	Yes, on the gross outstanding amount of certificates at less than 2 years
Monetary aggregates	M3–M2	L–M3 (3)	L–M3	M3–M2	M3–M2
Outstanding end-1988, share held by the public (1)	FRF 329.8 billion 77%	FRF 63 billion 97%	FRF 450 billion (4) 25%	FRF 34.2 billion 15%	FRF 23.9 billion 56%
Tax treatment	• Income: no deduction at source • Optional: withholding tax for physical persons at 32% (+ 2%). • Capital gains: treated in the same way as income.				

Notes: 1. Securities held by non-financial agents and undertakings for collective investment in transferable securities (UCITS).
2. For French franc-denominated certificates of deposit, at more than 1 year, reviewable rate possible as from the second year of duration.
3. Apart from commercial paper issued by the Caisse nationale des télécommunications, included in M3–M2.
4. Of which 432 billion of negotiable Treasury bills.

Certificates of Deposit

The development of certificates of deposit in francs was first slowed down by the requirement of a minimum maturity of six months, whereas the non-financial agents likely to subscribe to this paper preferred shorter maturities. This limitation has been abolished and starting 1 March 1987 CDs will cover a range of maturities from 10 days to 7 years. They are submitted to compulsory reserves in the liabilities of the banks.

At end 1989, the outstanding amount of certificates of deposit reached FRF 511 billion, equalling that of Treasury bills (FRF 520 billion). More than 75 per cent of this outstanding amount is held by the public.

Commercial Paper

Commercial paper can have maturities of 10 days to 7 years. This new instrument has been very successful. The total outstanding amount was FRF 129 billion by the end of December 1989, out of which FRF 124 billion were in the hands of non-banks.

Negotiable Treasury Bills

Issues of negotiable Treasury bills have been substantial. At the end of 1989, the outstanding amount of Treasury bills reached FRF 520 billion. Out of this total, FRF 126.5 billion only were in fact held by investment funds and non-financial agents.

The growth of the Treasury bill portfolio held by the public (non-financial agent and UCITS) is slower than that of certificates of deposit (FRF + 23 billion in 1989 compared with FRF + 142 billion). This is largely due to the strong demand for certificates of deposit from UCITS, entities that are very often linked up with banks. However, the creation of a network of 'primary dealers' to place the public debt was aimed in particular at broadening the range of customers, especially for Treasury bills.

Notes Issued by the Specialised Financial Institutions and Finance Companies

These bodies, which may not accept deposits from the public at less than two years, have been progressively authorised to issue notes with the same characteristics as bank certificates of deposit.

A total of FRF 39 billion of notes issued by specialised financial institutions was outstanding at the end of December 1989. Issues by finance companies reached FRF 37 billion.

5.2.5 The Interbank Market

Before it was reformed, the money market was open to some 'non-bank' entities which were thus able to obtain a market rate of return on all their investments. These included insurance companies, pension funds, the Stockbrokers' Board (*Chambre Syndicale des Agents de Change*) and the SICAVs; moreover, the volume of liquid assets held by the SICAVs had become considerable owing both to the growth of these bodies and to the fact that the liquidity ceiling applying to short-term SICAVs had been raised from 25 per cent to 40 per cent of their net assets at the end of 1984. The authorities' desire to support the spread of negotiable securities among the public and to restrict access to the market for 'central bank money' led it to mark out the boundaries of an interbank market proper, accessible only to credit institutions. In their liquidity management, the institutions which have been excluded from this interbank market have switched to repurchase agreements and purchases and sales of negotiable securities, which should help to promote the growth of the new markets of short-term securities.

5.2.6 The Financial Futures Markets

Opened on 20 February 1986, the financial futures market, or MATIF (*Marché à terme international de France*), initially dealt only in one long-term contract (denomination FRF 500,000) in a notional loan equivalent to a ten-year government loan, redeemable at maturity and bearing interest at 10 per cent. Any actual deliveries are in equivalent securities guaranteed by the government. In addition contracts in short-term Treasury bills have been traded since June.

Activity on the MATIF has surpassed the most optimistic forecasts since, instead of the 500 to 600 contracts expected per day, the number of contracts exchanged in the course of a normal trading session has rapidly increased and reached 60,500 during December 1989 (notional loans only).

Against the background of strong expectations of a fall in rates the speculators have been present in force on the MATIF, as buyers of contracts. Among them are to be found operators of all sizes and kinds, from the stockbroker's clerk to major industrial concerns, financial intermediaries, institutional investors and banks.

It is mainly the dealers who have been the sellers on the MATIF. They have been taking advantage of the discrepancies which are recorded daily between the futures market and the much more rigid spot market where the underlying securities are transacted. A spot transaction in effect presupposes substantial liquid funds and the actual delivery of paper, and it directly affects the operator's balance sheet, which is not the case with the futures market.

The MATIF sphere of activity has been gradually extended. Thus, in 1988, three new futures market products were created: the options contract on the notional loan, the three-month PIBOR contract and the CAC 40 index contract. With more than 17 million contracts in 1989, the French market ranks third world-wide, ahead of London.

The main operators are the financial institutions, brokerage firms and market makers (they account for more than 60 per cent of contracts). UCITS represent nearly a quarter of PIBOR contracts and 12 per cent of the notional contract whereas non-financial agents are seldom involved directly. Operations have become swiftly global, with non-residents accounting for nearly 25 per cent of Paris total amount for the notional loan and 20 per cent for the PIBOR contract. They are mainly citizens from the United States and Great Britain.

5.3 DISINTERMEDIATION

The financial institutions experienced a first wave of disintermediation in 1980 with the rapid growth of the long-term capital market, as already explained. For some months now they have been subjected to the repercussions of the creation of the markets in short-term negotiable instruments (commercial paper and negotiable Treasury bills).

5.3.1 The Wave of 1986: Commercial Paper and Negotiable Treasury Bills

By bringing the borrowers and lenders of short-term funds directly together, the development of commercial paper produced, ceteris paribus, a contraction both in bank lending to business firms and in non-financial sectors' bank deposits. Independently of its quantitative impact on the banks' assets and funding, the introduction of commercial paper had repercussions on:

1. lending terms in general,
2. the quality of banking risks.

In losing their monopoly in subscribing for Treasury bills bearing a market interest rate, and even more in losing a share of the short-term financing of companies issuing commercial paper, the banks are in the process of losing some of their least risky assets.

In addition to the deterioration in the general level of risk the banks have been confronted with a 'marketisation' process: as has also been observed in the United States, the increasing use of commercial paper against the background of a sharp decline in business financing requirements has heightened competition between financial institutions. A growing proportion of new bank loans are now granted at rates linked to the money market rate, with the banks taking only a comparatively narrow margin above this reference rate. It is estimated that 56 per cent of total outstanding credit to business firms is on terms linked to the money market rate rather than at the banks' base rate.

5.3.2 The Dismantling of Exchange Controls

Exchange controls have been progressively removed in France. Thus French companies can be expected to make growing use of the international financial techniques that have been a major factor in the growth of the international capital markets and the process of bank disintermediation.

In particular, they will be likely to use the new borrowing techniques that are substitutes for conventional loans at fixed or reviewable rates (issues of short-term paper, currency or interest rate swaps) as well as the techniques for hedging on the futures markets or in direct negotiation with bank or non-bank counterparties. (However, in 1989 the recourse to direct financing granted by non-residents does not seem to have increased further to a notable extent.)

As has happened in other countries, this can be expected to lead to an expansion of the banks' off-balance-sheet operations and further accentuate their service activities.

5.3.3   The Changing Share of Intermediated Financing in the Funding of the Economy

Since 1980 there has been a shift in the pattern of financial flows towards the capital market and away from bank intermediation.

In the 1970s the financial intermediaries provided almost 80 per cent of the funds raised by domestic non-financial sectors; their share decreased notably as from 1983, and reached an all-time low of 40 per cent in 1986.

Nevertheless the sharp fall in the intermediation ratio since 1980 is only in part attributable to the advance of the capital market; it also reflects an improvement in companies' financial and cash positions which is accompanied by a decline in recourse to short-term credit.

To compensate for the decline in their traditional intermediation role, banks sought to enlarge their household customer base, to whom they strongly increased their credits, mainly in the form of cash facilities. At the same time, the rise in corporate borrowing requirements, linked to the high level of productive investment and stock building, led firms to rely heavily again on bank credits. One therefore witnessed a marked increase in intermediation in 1987–1988, with its share up to 60 per cent in 1988. This recovery in intermediation shows that, in a period of rebounding economic activity, the additional financing requirement was mainly met by resorting to credits.

In all, of FRF 359 billion of disintermediated financing in 1989 only FRF 150 billion consisted of negotiable instruments, 65 per cent of which was in the form of bonds. Other direct funding was constituted by capital endowments and foreign investment.

II   IMPLICATIONS FOR MONETARY POLICY

The implementation of monetary policy is dependent on the structure of the financial system. Financial innovation has thus had the following consequences:

1. a redefinition of monetary aggregates;
   the need for qualification in interpreting monetary developments (because of variations in demand for money and velocity);
2. a change in the instruments of monetary policy (increased role of interest rates and corresponding decline of credit ceilings).

5.4 THE REDEFINITION OF MONETARY AGGREGATES

5.4.1 Methodological Rules in Force until 1985

The former aggregates were defined by the following criteria.

1. M3R, the broadest aggregate in France, comprised cash and assets which are easily convertible into means of payment without the holders incurring a risk of capital loss, irrespective of whether the conversion is anticipated or not, the only penalty being, in certain cases, a reduction of interest.
2. The assets falling within M3R were broken down according to liquidity or the type of institution with which they are deposited:

    (a) notes and checkable sight deposits came within M1;
    (b) liquid and short-term liabilities of banks were included in M2R – M1R, those of other financial institutions in M3R – M2R.

    M2R was the basis for monetary targeting.

5.4.2 The 1986 Reform

Monetary statistics are no longer split according to the kind of institution which acts as an intermediary. The breakdown is therefore mainly based on the type of investment.

A new, broad liquidity aggregate L includes, in addition to means of payment, all investment that non-financial agents consider to constitute an immediately available store of purchasing power because it can be converted easily and rapidly into means of payment without substantial risk of capital loss. A similar concept is used in the United Kingdom where 'assets which may be realised at short notice, with little actual or potential financial penalty (resulting from the forfeit of interest or from capital uncertainty)' are considered to be liquid assets (*source*: Bank of England).

5.5   THE CHANGE IN THE INSTRUMENTS OF MONETARY POLICY

5.5.1   The Decline of Direct Quantitative Credit Control Procedures

Credit ceilings are progressively dismantled in most countries, at least in their rigid form. In France, such a device only acted as a safety net in 1986 in order to ensure a transition to an interest rate policy, and was eliminated on 1 January 1987. In Japan, they have simply become 'the expression of the central bank's viewpoint on the short-term prospects of increasing credit'. In Italy, they have just been eliminated for the second half of 1986 after having been temporarily re-introduced during the first half of the year. This decline is the logical consequence of financial developments:

1. The development of alternative financing sources for companies (commercial paper, share and bond market and foreign loans where applicable) makes accurate control of bank credit alone an illusion.
2. The monetary financing of the budget deficit has become more difficult to plan *ex ante*. How would it be possible to determine in what proportion Treasury bill issues will contribute to swelling the portfolio of securities of non-financial agents rather than the portfolio of financial institutions?
3. The effectiveness of credit ceilings had in any case been weakened by the amount of unused margins available for new lending constituted by the banks during the year and the legislation had become fairly complex.

5.5.2   The Management of Market Interest Rates by the Central Bank

Conversely, interest rates are playing a major role and have become the main transmission mechanism in the French economy. Many factors explain this evolution, among which:

1. the share of the bank resources with a market interest rate has increased, since the credit ceiling system led them to issue debentures (see above);

2. bank credit and savings deposits compete with direct finance, so that their yield follows the market rates more closely;
3. deregulation and innovation make interest rates sensitive to capital supply and demand.

By intervening at the short-end of the capital market, the central bank is thus able to transmit the effects of its policy to the economy through the classical channels: portfolio choices, funds supply and demand, among which are bank credit supply and demand.

The circumstances made it feasible to shift from credit ceilings to market operations: inflation was around 2 per cent, the financial structure of the corporate sector was improving, the demand for credit was weakening (or growing less rapidly).

In December 1986, the Bank of France improved the functioning of the interbank market (with a continuous quotation) and its own techniques.

In practice, France which belongs to the European Exchange Rate Mechanism, does try to attain an exchange rate objective and a money supply target simultaneously. When a conflict arises between the two objectives, a priority has, of course, to be set, at least in the short term (in 1979 excessive money creation was tolerated in order to avoid an appreciation of the franc; in 1981–82 a destruction of money was allowed in order to combat the fall in the franc).

On a theoretical level there are two dominant views:

1. it is not possible to maintain a fixed exchange rate and an objective for money supply growth at the same time;
2. it is not possible to attain two objectives with a single instrument (in this instance, interest rates).

This is all the more true if exchange controls are dismantled, which is precisely what happened in France in 1986.

Experience shows that 'cohabitation' is a realistic issue – at least in France. Several preconditions have to be fulfilled. One is a good coherence between the quantitative targets of the money stock growth and what is aimed at on the exchange market. Another is to ensure a good convergence of fundamentals with the main partner countries. If it is not the case, some flexibility is required and the European Monetary System (EMS) provides some possibilities of this kind.

Note

* Most of the material used in this paper is taken directly from two contributions made on the same topic at the BIS economists' meeting of November 1986 and at the University of Illinois in September 1986 by Didier Bruneel, Director of Monetary Studies at the Banque de France.

6 Monetary Control in Japan

Tatsuya Tamura

The purpose of this paper is to explain *first* the background and mechanism of Japan's policy on monetary aggregates, *second* the changes in the monetary and financial system which began in the early 1980s and are still continuing, and *third* the implication of these changes for the Bank of Japan's current policy on the management of monetary aggregates.

6.1 MANAGEMENT OF MONETARY AGGREGATES IN JAPAN AFTER 1975

6.1.1 The Background to the Introduction of Money Supply Policy

The Bank of Japan officially announced it would introduce a so-called 'money supply policy' in July 1975. Already at that time, the central banks of the United States and the major European countries had shifted the emphasis of their monetary policies away from interest rates towards monetary aggregates, and the decision of Japan's central bank was another example of the way in which any central bank had to face the difficult economic situation of the mid-1970s.

The Bank of Japan explained this shift in the emphasis of the conduct of monetary policy *from* interest rates *to* monetary aggregates as follows:

> In order to achieve price stability and to strive for the appropriate development of the economy, it will be necessary to pay sufficient attention in the future to the movements of M2 in the management of monetary policy . . . In the actual management of policy, the growth rate of the money supply should be kept stable in cases when it is judged that no particularly large economic problems loom, and in cases when problems do loom the reasons for these problems should be analysed and a realistic monetary policy

101

attitude should be adopted, which continuously reconsiders policy management in the direction of correcting future growth rates of the money supply. Monetary aggregate oriented monetary policy, however, in no way implies decreased importance for interest rate policy. Rather, in order to achieve effectiveness in quantitative adjustments, it is absolutely necessary that interest rate policy be managed in a way that is consistent with the underlying tenor of quantitative adjustment policy.

The purpose of this statement was to give the money supply a place as an intermediate objective for conducting monetary policy. But it was not until July 1978 that the Bank of Japan began to announce to the public some quantitative figures which indicated the policy intentions of the central bank. Since that time, the Bank of Japan has made it a rule to announce, at the beginning of every quarter, an estimate of the growth rate of the monetary aggregate during the quarter compared with the same period of the previous year. This procedure has not changed up to now and the figure for monetary growth is called a 'forecast'. Originally, the definition of the money supply used for the 'forecast' was M2 (that is money in circulation plus demand and time deposits with the commercial banks), but the definition was changed to M2 + CDs in 1979 when the latter began to be issued.

In retrospect the reasons why the Bank of Japan had to shift emphasis on to monetary aggregates could be explained as follows. The first was the increased difficulty in distinguishing just exactly what information interest rate movements were giving about the effectiveness of monetary policy. This difficulty emerged from the gradual inflation in late 1960s, followed by the intensified worldwide inflation after the first oil shock. For example, when interest rates rise, it is not possible to judge decisively whether this rise has occurred because of higher inflationary expectations, because of the increase in money demand over money supply generated by over-heating of the business cycle, or because of a decrease in money supply as the effects of a tighter monetary policy permeate through the economy. If either of the first two reasons is valid then there is a need to tighten monetary policy further; but if the latter is the case then there is no such need. An indicator that does not allow such differentiation of judgements is inappropriate as an intermediate guide for monetary policy.

The second reason for shifting emphasis concerns Japan's experiences during the early 1970s. As a result of the excess money supply growth during 1971 to 1972 (the peak rates of money supply growth for M1 and M2 were about 30 per cent in a year), consumer price inflation rose to above ten per cent during the period 1973 to 1975. In order to overcome this inflation, the Japanese economy had to endure a long and painful adjustment process until 1977. The battle against inflation became a major concern for the Japanese public.

The third reason was a change in the flow of funds inside the Japanese economy. On the one hand, the corporate sector reduced their demand for funds, reflecting the slowdown in economic growth, and on the other hand the government sector registered a huge increase in their demand for funds (that is, the large scale flotation of government bonds). As a result, the channels of creation of the money supply were no longer limited to increases in the commercial banks' lending to the private sector, but now included the thick pipe of banks' underwriting of government bonds. The supply of money created from banks' underwriting of government bonds accumulated and this improved the liquidity position of private sectors. It thus became possible for the corporate sector to expand investment without relying on bank lending. The money stock therefore became an important indicator – rather than bank lending to the private sector – when we judge the level of aggregate expenditure. In a sense, after 1975 it became necessary to use the money supply itself as the intermediate monetary policy objective, and the bank lending figures, which served fairly well for a policy objective, became a partial indicator.

6.1.2 Monetary Targeting à la Japonaise

Choice of Monetary Indicator

The Bank of Japan employs broadly defined money – that is M2 + CDs – as its most important monetary indicator. One reason is that, as past statistics reveal, the movement of M2 + CDs *leads* the movements of income and expenditure. M1 has a closer statistical relationship with income and expenditure, but it does not *lead* income and expenditure.

A second reason for using M2 + CDs is its superior controllability. The central bank's ability to exert a short-term control over base money or M1 is quite limited because of M1's close relationship with current income and expenditure. The short-term shifts of funds between bank notes and demand deposits or between demand and time deposits are unpredictable and difficult to control. With respect to M2 + CDs, however, such shifts between various types of deposits are only compositional shifts within the definition of the money supply, so that if the central bank can control the total amount of credit granted by commercial banks then the movement of M2 + CDs is under control.

In addition, the figures on M2 + CDs have a high degree of statistical accuracy and reporting lags are as short as the figures of base money or M1.

The Period over which Control is Exerted

The problem of the period over which to set the monetary target is not independent of the problem of which indicator to choose. It has become a rule that the Bank of Japan makes an announcement, in the first month of each quarter, of the estimate of the rate of increase of M2 + CDs in the current quarter compared with the corresponding period of the previous year. In this sense, the rate of increase during the past year is the focus of attention. The reasoning behind this is that the current levels of income, expenditure, and prices are influenced by movements in the money supply with the lag of approximately the previous two years. Thus, it is important to exert appropriate control over the money supply for periods of a year or more rather than just for short periods of a month or a quarter.

Determination and Announcement of the Intermediate Objective

The Bank of Japan focuses on M2 + CDs but does not announce 'targets' in a strict sense of the word. Only 'forecasts' are announced. However, the policy actions of the Bank of Japan itself are included in the determination of these 'forecasts' and in this sense the forecasts represent movement of the money supply that the Bank of Japan is willing to permit. The Bank of Japan continuously pays close attention to the effects that the trends of money supply growth will have on future income, expenditure, and prices. When undesirable movements in money supply are recognised monetary policy actions will be taken. At such times the 'forecasts' include the effect of policy changes (that is, they should show gradual moves in the desirable direction). In Table 6.1, a comparison of the 'forecasts' announced

Table 6.1   Japanese money supply forecasts, 1978–89 (in percentage changes over previous year)

		Forecast	Actuals
1978	July–Sep.	It is most likely to grow over 11%, should it turn to be on the higher side it may be around 12%	12.1
	Oct–Dec.	12.0–12.9	12.2
1979	Jan–Mar.	12.0–12.9	12.3
	Apr–June	12.0–12.9	12.1
	July–Sep.	around 12	11.7
	Oct–Dec.	around 11	11.2
1980	Jan–Mar.	around 10	10.6
	Apr–June	10.0–10.9	10.1
	July–Sep.	slightly less than 10	8.4
	Oct–Dec.	around 8	7.8
1981	Jan–Mar.	around 7	7.6
	Apr–June	7.0–7.9	7.9
	July–Sep.	9.0–9.9	9.6
	Oct–Dec.	10.0–10.9	10.6
1982	Jan–Mar.	around 11	10.6
	Apr–June	around 10	9.2
	July–Sep.	around 9	9.0
	Oct–Dec.	around 8	8.1
1983	Jan–Mar.	7.0–7.9	7.6
	Apr–June	7.0–7.9	7.6
	July–Sep.	around 7	7.1
	Oct–Dec.	around 7	7.2
1984	Jan–Mar.	7.0–7.9	7.9
	Apr–June	around 8	7.6
	July–Sep.	around 8	7.8
	Oct–Dec.	around 8	7.9
1985	Jan–Mar.	around 8	7.9
	Apr–June	around 8	8.3
	July–Sep.	around 8	8.3
	Oct–Dec.	8.0–8.9	9.0
1986	Jan–Mar.	around 9	9.0
	Apr–June	It is most likely to grow over 8%, should it turn to be on the higher side it may be around 9%	
	July–Sep.	8.0–8.9	8.8
	Oct–Dec.	most likely 8.0–8.9	8.3
1987	Jan–Mar.	around 8	8.8
	Apr–June	around 9	10.0
	July–Sep.	around 10	10.8
	Oct–Dec.	11.0–11.9	11.8

continued on page 106

Table 6.1 *continued*

		Forecast	Actuals
1988	Jan–Mar.	around 12	12.1
	Apr–June	around 12	11.3
	July–Sep.	10.0–10.9	10.9
	Oct–Dec.	10.0–10.9	10.6
1989	Jan–Mar.	10.0–10.9	10.3
	Apr–June	10.0–10.9	9.7
	July–Sep.	9.0–9.9	9.7

Note: Money supply represents M2 up to April–June 1979, and M2 + CDs thereafter.

by the Bank of Japan and actual growth rates of M2 + CDs shows that our forecasts are in fact very close to actual growth.

6.1.3 How Money Supply is Managed

During the 1960s and early 1970s, when government bond floatation was negligible, the Bank of Japan heavily depended upon so called 'window guidance' to manage the total volume of bank credit. But during this period, at the same time, a new market oriented channel of transmission of monetary policy gradually developed. The following shows how money markets function in Japan and how monetary policy pulses are transmitted to the entire economy through market mechanisms.

Interbank Interest Rates as Operating Variables

For the Bank of Japan, the operating variables for daily management have always been interbank interest rates. By market intervention we aim to attain intermediate objectives like the total volume of bank credit, or the growth of monetary aggregate such as M2 + CDs.

The ability of the Bank of Japan to control interbank interest rates as a means of day-to-day monetary adjustment is based on its ability to affect demand and supply conditions for funds in the interbank market through its lending policy and bill operations. At a more technical level the Bank of Japan's ability to control interest rates is based on its ability to affect the path along which reserves are accumulated. Under the reserve requirement system in Japan, required reserve levels are based on average deposits over a period of one calendar month, but the reserves could be accumulated (in Bank of Japan deposits) from the 16th of this month to the 15th of the following month. It is the average level of reserves during this period that counts in calculating banks' compliance with the reserve requirements: but the actual outstanding amount of reserve deposits may vary from day to day. If, for example, repayment of Bank of Japan loans or other factors causes a decrease of reserves in the system so that the level of reserve deposits at the central bank continues for several days to be less than the required level, then the so-called 'reserves accumulation path' gradually falls behind schedule. As a result, the financial institutions will begin to look for reserve funds in the interbank market. The gap between demand and supply will gradually become larger, and interbank market interest rates will rise. Of course, if on one day a huge swing of demand for reserve money causes the reserve deposits for the banking system as a whole to become negative, then a bank somewhere in the system would have fallen into default, and credit conditions would become disorderly. In order to avoid such situation the Bank of Japan of course acts as the lender of last resort. Even without forcing reserves to such a low level, however, a delay in the reserve accumulation path can cause interest rates in the market to rise gradually. On the other hand, it is also possible for the Bank of Japan to induce the accumulation of reserves through lump-sum purchases of bills. In such cases the demand – supply situation in the interbank market gradually becomes easier and interest rates begin to fall.

Influence of Interbank Market Interest Rates on the Money Supply

Let me now explain the process by which the operating variables of interbank interest rates affect the intermediate objectives of the money supply.

Changes in the interbank market rates affect the money supply primarily through three channels: (1) effects on the banks' loan decisions, (2) financial disintermediation, and (3) effects of interest rate changes on the expenditures of individuals and corporations. The first of these was the traditional transmission channel during the post-war high growth period, while the second and third are channels that have become important with the development of open markets and the more flexible movement of interest rates in these markets. Let me describe the transmission mechanism of policy changes through each of these three channels in the case of an increase in interbank interest rates due to a tightening of monetary policy.

First come the effects of the interest rate increase on the banks' decisions on their loan business. Although interest rates on loans in Japan are not regulated, they tend to be sticky because of (1) the *de facto* link between prime rates and the official discount rate, and (2) the difficulty of suddenly changing interest rates, when the banks prize their long-term customer relationships. In addition, the terms of issue of corporate bonds were inflexible for a long period and did not reflect the cost of funds. Thus, both lending rates and bond subscriber yields could become unattractive compared with interbank interest rates, which usually rise much more than the official discount rate. Banks and other financial institutions naturally reduce their lending and absorption of bonds. Financial institutions tend to increase their placement of funds in the interbank markets, or at least to repay what they have borrowed in the interbank market. (The resultant easing of the demand–supply balance in the interbank market would be absorbed without delay by further Bank of Japan money market operations). As a result, extension of credit to the private sector would be reduced and the availability of credit falls simultaneously, leading to a reduction in economic activity of the corporate sector (which used to depend heavily on external funds). This is nothing other than a reduction in spending due to a fall in the money supply. Window guidance on bank lending to the private sector supplements this mechanism and has the effect of quickening the speed of asset adjustment by the banks.

Higher interbank interest rates could also cause financial disintermediation. The regulated interest rates on bank deposits were relatively low in comparison to the yields of financial assets that became available in the open money markets. The result was that the nonbank sector (such as large corporations) could shift its financial assets to a certain extent from deposits to the free market instruments, although the volume to begin with was limited. As a result, banks began to suffer shortage of deposits and found it difficult to extend credit. If the customers who are no longer able to get bank credit are able to raise equivalent amounts from the open markets, then there is no tightening of financial conditions. However, small and medium-sized businesses and individuals do have limited access to the open market, so their monetary condition tighten.

The third effect of interbank interest rates changes is their direct influence on private expenditure. Rises in interbank money market rates invite rises in open market interest rates such as the *gensaki* (short-term repurchase agreement on bonds), CDs and secondary bond markets through interest rates arbitrage between these instruments and interbank instruments. The pressure for higher interest rates eventually reaches even the banks' sticky lending rates and corporate bond subscription rates. These increases constitute improvements in financial investment yields for sectors of the economy with surplus funds, and also constitute increases in fund raising costs for deficit sectors. In other words, the opportunity cost of investment rises for surplus sectors while the borrowing cost of investment rises for deficit sectors. Both of these changes tend to reduce investment activity and thus income. As a result, demand for money falls and the money stock is reduced.

6.1.4 The Japanese Economy since 1975

Figure 6.1 shows the difference in the movements of money supply, nominal GNP, and real GNP for the periods before and after 1975, when monetary aggregates began to play an important role in monetary policy. The period after 1975 has four characteristics. First, the average rate of growth of the money supply became much lower than in previous years and variations have been within 5 per cent of the average rate of growth. Secondly, the rate of growth of nominal GNP is declining and its variability is getting smaller. Thirdly, the growth rate of real GNP has been around a 5 per cent level except in 1981–83 when there was a worldwide recession. Fourthly, as a result of the two previous factors, the inflation rate – as measured by the GNP deflator – has also fallen in recent years to 1 to 2 per cent.

These movements of macroeconomic indicators contrast clearly with those in the period up to 1974. In the earlier period, the growth rate of money supply ranged from 15 to 25 per cent, a very wide band. Growth rates of nominal GNP also fluctuated widely as did the real GNP. In addition, the average rate of inflation, measured by the GNP deflator, was as high as 6 per cent.

The difference of performance in the Japanese economy before and after 1975 could be attributed to a certain extent to differences in the way monetary policy was conducted. The good performance of the Japanese economy since 1975 is particularly interesting considering the many external shocks that occurred during this period. I am thinking here of growing volatility of exchange rates, the second oil crisis, the subsequent worldwide inflation, the simultaneous recession

110

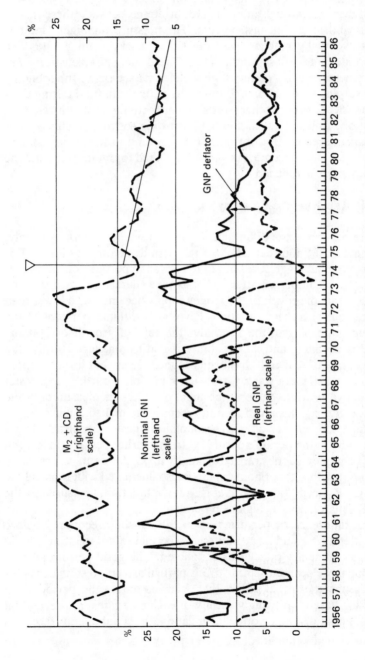

Figure 6.1   Money supply and GNP in Japan, 1956–86 (percentage change from same period of previous year)
Note: For M2 + CDs, average of amounts outstanding at month-end, for the period before Q1 1979, M2.

in its aftermath and the deepening of the debt crisis. The Japanese economy stayed reasonably stable in this difficult environment when some major countries could not avoid large disturbances.

6.2 STRUCTURAL CHANGES IN JAPANESE FINANCIAL MARKETS

The decade from 1975 was at the same time the period when Japanese money and capital markets and its financial institutions experienced the sort of major structural changes which take place once every 50 or 100 years.

6.2.1 The Deregulation of Interest Rates on Newly Issued Government Bonds

The fiscal year 1975 was the first in which the Japanese government suffered a large drop in tax revenue, caused by the worldwide recession that followed the oil crisis. This also induced pressure for structual changes because of the need to float a huge amount of government debt.

As the volume of government bond issues grew, the prevailing system of issues via underwriting syndicates at below-market rates could no longer work smoothly. During the mid-1970s a gap emerged between the yields of new issues and the yields on the secondary markets as the volume of issues mushroomed so that interest rate negotiations between the government and the syndicates often failed to reach agreement. As a result, the government in 1978 began to issue, by public tender, 2 to 4 year medium-term government bonds. From 1986 the government began public tender of short-term government bonds. That is to say, interest rates in this part of the *primary market* for government bonds have been liberalised and are freely determined by the market. As these interest rates are higher than regulated savings instruments of similar maturities (time deposits, money trusts, loan trusts, and so on) personal savings began to flow out of financial institutions into government bonds.

This shift of funds, or disintermediation, was accelerated by another financial innovation from securities companies; the 'Chuki-Kokusai fund', introduced in 1980, which specialises in investments of medium-term government bonds. This kind of investment trust was designed so that it could be converted into cash any time after the initial 30 days. At the same time its yield was much higher than that on similar bank deposits (such as saving deposits). Therefore it attracted substantial funds from both the personal and corporate sectors. This financial instrument is similar to money-market mutual funds in the United States. In addition, securities companies began to offer other new investment funds such as the 'Rikin fund', a form of short-term investment trust that makes use of interest income derived from bonds, and the 'Kokusai fund' which specialises in high yield government bonds available in the secondary market. Because of the introduction of these new products investment trusts have grown rapidly in the 1980s.

6.2.2 Deregulation of Banking Instruments

As disintermediation of bank deposits continued, regulations imposed on banks began to be partly liberalised. From 1979 onwards, banks were permitted to issue individual CDs (negotiable certificates of deposit) worth at least Yen 500 million (about £2 million), subject to a quantitative ceiling that total issues must not exceed 10 per cent of broadly-defined net worth. The minimum amount was lowered to Yen 100 million in April 1985 and the quantitative ceiling has been gradually raised to 300 per cent of net worth (by April 1987). As a result, although banks are still subject to the quantitative ceiling, it has become possible for them to offer high interest rates for large certificates of deposits. Although interest rates on time deposits of smaller amounts have always been regulated, since 1981 banks have been allowed to offer higher yield new products to small savers. Commercial banks began to sell 'maturity-designated time deposits' of up to three years. Trust banks and long-term credit banks have been permitted to offer a special type of high yield five-year loan trust called 'Big', and bank debentures of five years called 'Wide'. All three types of instrument offer high yields by compound interest arrangements, and can easily be converted to cash at the issuing banks before maturity. Since 1983, banks have been allowed to begin some securities business; for instance, they began to sell newly-issued medium and long-term government bonds over the counter. Japanese banks took advantage of this opportunity to offer new saving instruments such as 'government bond time deposit accounts' (Kokusai-teiki-koza) or 'government bond trust accounts' (Kokusai-shintaku-koza). In these accounts, newly-issued bonds are held in custody with banks, with the interest obtained on them transferred automatically to time deposit or money trust accounts at the banks (so that the interest income for government bonds yields compound interest).

Furthermore, in March 1985 banks were permitted to issue six-month non-negotiable money market certificates, so called MMCs, of at least Yen 50 million, and this minimum was lowered to Yen 20 million in April 1987. The interest rate of this instrument is regulated but the level was always kept very close to money market rates. Also, the interest rate ceiling on large-denomination time deposits (from Yen 1 billion) was removed in October 1985, and the minimum amount of this deposit was gradually reduced to Yen 100 million by April 1987. Additionally, the maximum maturity of both CDs and MMCs was extended from six months to one year and two years respectively.

6.2.3 Deregulation of International Financial Activities

Since the transition to the floating exchange rate system in 1973, the domestic and international financial markets have become more and more integrated. This was another reason for the above-mentioned liberalisation of domestic interest rates and financial transactions. Liberalisation of international financial transactions was accelerated by changes abroad. First came the liberalisation of interest rates on foreign currency deposits in 1974 which really marked the first step in the deregulation of deposit interest rates in Japan. Indeed, at that time the holding of foreign currency accounts by Japanese residents required a licence. However, since 1975 foreign currency holdings up to the equivalent of Yen 3 million were permitted; in 1980 this ceiling was totally removed. Then, borrowing by Japanese residents in foreign currencies (impact loans) from markets abroad, directly or through Japanese banks, was completely liberalised. At the same time, the holding of foreign securities by residents, as well as investment in domestic securities by non-residents, was freed.

International financial transactions of this kind, as well as deregulation of financial transactions in the domestic securities markets, provided the impetus to the liberalisation of domestic financial transactions as whole.

6.2.4 The Impact of Technological Innovation

Structual changes have also stemmed from micro-electronic and telecommunication developments which have lowered information and management costs in financial markets. As a result of this, various financial innovations have occurred in transacting accounts, and progress has been made in economising on currency and demand deposits.

Examples of innovations which have helped to economise cash holdings of individuals are: (1) payment by personal credit cards, (2) automatic transfer of salaries to bank accounts, (3) payment of public utility charges by automatic transfer (new settlement practices have been made possible by development of the in-bank on-line computer network), (4) establishment of a system of deposit withdrawals through cash dispensers and automated teller machines since 1975 (which were made possible by the formation of a network of on-line computer systems among banks).

On the other hand, economising on demand deposits was helped by the establishment of the 'combined deposit account' so called 'So-go-koza'. This account provides for the granting of automatic overdrafts using time deposits or loan trusts as collateral whenever the balance in a demand deposit account is not enough for a certain payment. In fact, this allows financial investment instruments to perform the transaction function.

Table 6.2 shows outstanding amounts, and rates of growth of different types of monetary assets between 1981 and 1986. We find that traditional financial assets such as sight deposits or time deposits have grown at a very low rate and new assets such as unregulated interest-bearing time deposits or foreign currency deposits have become very important in the short run.

6.3 IMPLICATION FOR MONETARY POLICY

The implication for monetary policy of these structural changes in the financial environment is fairly mixed and complicated.

6.3.1 Effects on the Demand for Money

As far as traditionally defined M1 is concerned, many new products and innovations have combined to economise on currency in circulation and non-interest-bearing demand deposits at banks. Cash dispensers, automatic teller machines, credit cards and the above-mentioned So-go-koza account are typical of these developments.

Table 6.2   Changes in various types of Japanese financial assets between 1980 and 1986 (¥ trillion, average outstanding in 4th quarter)

	1980	1986	($ bill.)	% change (86/80)
1. Notes & coin in circulation	15.0	22.2	(147.8)	48.0
2. Sight deposits with banks	50.4	67.9	(452.8)	34.7
3. Postal Savings ordinary deposits	5.7	8.4	(55.9)	47.4
4. Sight deposits with Cooperatives, etc.	8.1	11.1	(74.4)	37.0
5. Regulated-interest-bearing time deposits with banks	134.1	200.4	(1336.0)	49.4
6. Unregulated-interest-bearing time deposits with banks	3.1	40.2	(267.9)	1196.8
of which,				
a. CDs	2.1	8.7	(57.7)	314.3
b. MMCs	–	7.8	(52.4)	–
c. Large denomination time deposits	–	16.1	(107.2)	–
d. Foreign currency deposits	1.0	7.6	(50.6)	660.0
7. Postal Savings certificates	52.3	98.9	(659.0)	89.1
8. Time deposits with cooperatives, etc.	30.4	48.8	(325.3)	60.5
9. TBs	–	1.0	(6.8)	–
10. RPs	3.8	4.7	(31.4)	23.7
11. Mid-term government bond funds	0.2	5.2	(34.8)	2500.0
12. Discount bank debentures	8.3	15.9	(106.0)	91.6
13. Short-term government securities	–	1.6	(10.4)	–
14. Fixed-rated bank debentures	8.1	14.1	(93.7)	74.1
15. Government bonds (excluding TBs & short-term securities)	14.7	23.4	(156.2)	59.2
16. Bond investment trusts	1.7	7.0	(46.8)	311.8
17. Stock investment trusts	3.8	15.9	(106.4)	318.4
18. Foreign bonds	0.1	7.9	(52.6)	7800.0
19. Outstanding principals in trust	21.9	40.9	(272.4)	86.8
20. Money deposited other than money in trust	0.1	3.1	(20.8)	3000.0

Notes: Definitions of Japanese monetary indicators:
M1 = 1+2 (notes and coin in circulation and sight deposits with banks)
M2 + CDs = M1 + 5 + 6 (M1 and regulated- and unregulated-interest-bearing time deposits with banks)

	1980	1986	($ bill.)	% change (86/80)
1. M1	65.4	90.1	(600.6)	37.8
2. M2 + CDs	202.6	330.7	(2204.5)	63.2

As to M2 (mainly time and saving deposits at banks), developments are two way. Introduction of CDs, MMCs or deregulation of large time deposits are factors which make time deposits at banks competitive and contribute to the recovery of bank intermediation. So-go accounts, which make time deposits work as if they were liquid demand deposits, also contributed to the growth of bank time deposits. On the other hand, numerous new products and innovations carried by securities companies were all to contribute to disintermediate or to decrease demand for time deposits. The most powerful are the Chuki-kokusai funds (medium-term government bond funds). Furthermore, although they are neither an innovation nor a new product, government bonds now carry more attractive interest rates compared with banks' time deposits, and have become a more and more important substitute for claims on banks.

These developments caused some kind of structural shift in the demand-for-money function. In theory, this shift could have been statistically separated from cyclical movements in the demand for money, but in practice, these structural changes were taking place at irregular intervals and with unpredictable strengths, so that the demand-for-money function would tend to be statistically less significant.

6.3.2 The Problem of Defining Money

Because of all the innovations contributing to less demand for currency and demand deposits, we would expect the growth rate of M1 to decline and variations in it should gradually become smaller. As a result, it may lose its meaning as an indicator of the volume of transactions in the economy.

As for M2, as new products or innovations increase, attributes such as the maturity or liquidity of financial assets become more complex and attempts to draw a line inevitably becomes arbitrary. Institutions which offer these financial assets have become more and more widespread. For example, I am thinking of life insurance policies which can offer effective interest to participants at rates close to money market rates. They are obviously to some extent a substitute for traditional time deposits. Foreign financial institutions are also beginning to offer financial assets (such as Euro-yen deposits) which could be a complete substitute for traditionally defined money.

In these circumstances it is very difficult to define clearly separate categories of money supply and compile monetary aggregate statistics without either delay or important leakages.

6.3.3 Changes in the Transmission Mechanism of Monetary Policy

Structural changes in the financial system which took place in the last decade are naturally accompanied by changes in the transmission mechanism of monetary policy. At the time when a money-supply-oriented policy was introduced, three major channels of transmission were expected to operate; namely (1) reaction of banks to changes in the cost of money raised in the market relative to loan yield, (2) disintermediation caused by the discrepancy of interest rates between regulated deposits and liberalised financial assets such as GENSAKI, (3) adjustment of expenditure by individuals and firms reflected in changes in the yield on financial assets compared with real assets.

Of these channels, the first two presuppose some rigidity or regulation of interest rates. As deregulation of interest rates and the liberalisation of financial products proceed, these two channels are becoming less important. Interest rates on bank loans, which move slowly with changes in the prime rate (which, in turn, is tied to the official discount rate), are becoming more flexible and realistic through the introduction of 'spread banking'. Spread banking means the pricing of bank loans according to a well-agreed formula which is based on the cost of funding, for example, the interbank rate plus a certain fixed margin.

As deregulations continue and the free movement of interest rates becomes predominant, monetary policy will be channelled more and more through the third channel. It becomes increasingly difficult to control M2 from the supply side, through movements of market interest rates, compared to past experience. Money supply becomes more dependent on the decision of individuals and corporations as they adjust their financial and real assets to changes in their financial conditions.

6.4 CONCLUSION

These developments, which might eventually undermine the basic reasoning behind a money-supply-oriented policy, have not yet completely taken place. The deregulation of interest rates on bank deposit has encompassed only one quarter of the volume of bank deposits (even for the major banks). Bank loans based on spread banking principle are still a small portion of total loans. Euro-yen holdings by Japanese residents are not completely liberalised and the total amount is still negligible (at present Euro-yen assets held by Japanese residents are estimated at less than one per cent of M2 + CDs).

Under these circumstances, the Bank of Japan has not yet changed the monetary policy strategy which it established in the mid 1970s. More careful attention is now being paid to the interpretation of movements of the monetary aggregate and its implication for future movements of prices and incomes. The Bank of Japan continues to announce forecasts of M2 + CDs in almost the same way as it began back in 1978.

As for recent movements of the money supply the Bank of Japan's assessment is as follows:

The rate of money supply growth remains at a high level despite the deceleration of economic activity. M2 + CDs, which is the main indicator of monetary aggregates, has accelerated since spring 1985. In both October–December 1985 and January–March 1986, M2 + CDs increased at a high annual rate of 9.0 per cent. Although it slowed temporarily, to 8.5 per cent in April–June, M2 + CDs began to accelerate again from mid 1986. For the January–March quarter 1987 rate of growth was at 8.8 per cent, and for April 9.8 per cent.

It appears that two factors are at work; one is the improvement in the competitiveness of financial assets – defined as time deposits – after the liberalisation of various deposit interest rates, including the introduction of MMCs and large-denomination time deposits; the other is the reduction of interest rates, especially since 1985 which lowered the opportunity of holding non-interest-bearing transaction money, such as currency or demand deposits.

To forestall questions on whether or not the current liquidity is excessive, it should be borne in mind, that reflecting the continued growth of M2 + CDs at a faster rate than nominal gross national product, the *velocity* of M2 + CDs, as measured by their proportion of total nominal demand, has declined more rapidly since November 1980 than in the previous period of monetary relaxation. Secondly, the growth of total liquidity in the economy, including the flourishing investment trust and foreign and domestic bonds, has remained high (9.0 – 9.5 per cent), although it has not accelerated as much as M2 + CDs. Therefore, careful attention should be paid to monetary conditions as the total liquidity is growing at a considerably high speed relative to the growth of total nominal demand.

The higher the level of liquidity, the greater is the danger that accumulated financial assets may turn into speculative investment in real assets. The recent surge in land and other real estate prices in Japan seems to be related to the high level of liquidity. Though stability in the general level of prices, as measured by the consumer price index or the GNP deflator, can be expected to continue for the time being and Japan's economic activity is gradually decelerating, closer attention than ever should be paid to the level of liquidity in order to prevent the rekindling of inflationary expectations in a period of historically low interest rates.

At the same time in the Bank of Japan, an intensive review of issues concerning money, income and central banking is under way. At this stage I cannot predict what the conclusion of this review will be, but we do completely share the following remarks of Governor Leigh-Pemberton in his 1986 lecture at Loughborough University:

> Whatever the outcome of that review, of one thing I am quite certain: it would be just as unwise to pay insufficient regard to the behaviour of broad money – on the grounds that that behaviour can change through time and is always difficult to interpret and understand – as it would be to place too much or too precise emphasis upon it. The detailed study of liquidity and of the development of credit are essential elements in judging financial conditions, even though they cannot be and never have been, the sole element.

References

Osugi, K. (1990), 'Japan's Experience of Financial Deregulation since 1984 in an International Perspective', *BIS Economic Papers*, no. 26, January.

Suzuki, Y. (1984) 'Financial Innovation and Monetary Policy in Japan', *Bank of Japan, Monetary and Economic Studies*, 2, 1, June 1984.

Suzuki, Y. (ed.) (1988) *The Japanese Financial System* (Oxford: Oxford University Press).

7 Financial Innovation: A View from the Bank of England

John S. Flemming

7.1 INTRODUCTION

There are many candidates for consideration as financial innovations: medium-term floating rate credits, floating rate instruments, financial futures, securitisation, new hedging instruments and techniques, and so on. There is scope for argument as to which of these developments were, and which were not, truly innovatory. Several of them reflect shifts in the relative roles of the banking system and the capital market in mediating between ultimate lenders and borrowers. Inflation and its uncertainty, and the associated varying uncertainty about nominal interest rates, have played a large part here. Swaps between currencies and maturities can also be seen as a natural development of back-to-back loans and indeed acceptance credits which have been around for many years.

I intend for the most part to take a narrower and more parochial view of innovation, perhaps in the econometric sense of an innovation as something not merely new but unexpectedly so and thus constituting 'news'. I shall therefore focus in the first place on changes in the domestic credit market brought about by policy changes since 1979. These fall into two categories. The first in time was the abolition of exchange controls in 1979. The second, with which I start, is the set of regulatory changes which have between 1980 and 1986 put banks and building societies progressively on a much more even footing and have tended to break down the separation of the mortgage market from that for other forms of personal credit.

That story is the subject of Part 7.2. In Part 7.3 I look ahead to the possible conclusion of this process. I then turn to the development of hedging techniques, the resort to which, in their international form, was facilitated by the ending of exchange control.

In the final part (7.4) I look at the implications for the prospects of the system and its reaction to policy measures of the freer access of households to credit and of the greater prevalence of hedged positions.

7.2 BANKS AND BUILDING SOCIETIES

Banks and building societies have co-existed in Britain for over one hundred years. They used to differ in several respects: building societies were mutual societies unlike the profit-making joint-stock banks – indeed they are subject to the registrar of 'friendly societies'. Their lending, apart from holdings of liquid, largely government, debt, has been concentrated on first mortgages on residential property. Since 1915, when they were caught by rent controls, this has been restricted largely to owner-occupied property – a growing sector of the UK market. Until about 1960 most of these mortgages would have been at fixed rates for about 20 years; this distinguished building societies sharply from banks lending on overdraft. Medium-term bank lending to companies has grown since building societies abandoned fixed rate lending. Building society depositors traditionally came from different strata of society than bank customers; the deposits were not chequable, partly because the societies were not, until very recently, allowed to make any unsecured advances. With hindsight one can see this process of convergence between the two types of business as having started many years ago but it is not surprising that when definitions of money were being formulated building societies were excluded from the monetary sector.

For many years before 1980 banks had been subject to guidance in their lending, and at times to restrictions as well, which had kept them out of the domestic residential mortgage market, apart from a temporary foray in 1972–73. Given a relatively free hand in that market the mutual building societies had chosen collectively to smooth the interest rate chargeable on their variable rate mortgages. Their motive for doing this is not entirely clear. As mutuals they may not have been very sensitive to missed profit opportunities; but the opportunities foregone were opportunities for *mutually* beneficial transactions. It is not clear why, as self-conscious instruments of social progress, they denied their prospective customers these opportunities.

It is of course true that, in the case of interest rate increases, existing borrowers' interests may have prevailed over those of prospective borrowers, but some asymmetry is required to explain the switch from a concern for existing borrowers which retarded rate rises, to a concern for existing lenders which retarded rate falls. It may be that the obligations on the societies, unlike banks lending on overdrafts, to notify their customers individually in advance of rate changes made rate changes more costly, particularly before computers became standard equipment, and thus rationalised rate smoothing. The cost argument, however, would not have required a cartel for the implementation of a smoothed structure. Be that as it may there was a cartel, rates were smoothed, and periods of excess demand were met by rationing. The societies could ration simply by queuing until such times as rate relativities and cash flows adjusted, or they could lend a lower multiple of borrowers' incomes or of the value of the property offered as security.

This system has collapsed progressively and in a fairly orderly manner since 1980, with banks taking a substantial share of the market and with an end to rationing although, of course, lenders continue to observe limits related to borrowers' income and collateral while, for the most part, lending on standardised terms. Moreover until the end of 1986 both banks and building societies were subject to some restraints on extending top-up mortgages on first mortgage terms.

The banks' invasions of the mortgage market have been associated with widely advertised special offers while the building societies have actively promoted various special deposits. The effect of these various promotions on the inflows and outflows of the societies has made it increasingly important to them that they have been able, since 1983, to raise funds on the wholesale money market (although subject to restrictions not applied to banks).

Another element in the equalisation of treatment of the two sets of institutions was the extension in 1985 of the Composite Rate Tax system to interest payable on retail bank deposits. This is an irrecoverable withholding tax at a rate slightly below the basic rate of income tax. The effect was to make the interest rates quoted on bank and building society deposits strictly comparable. A number of banks have responded by introducing a variety of interest paying accounts against which relatively high denomination cheques can be written at various restricted intervals. These accounts are somewhat similar to the various high interest variable notice accounts of the building societies.

I shall refrain from giving a rehearsal of effects of these various measures, and the institutions' responses, on their several shares of mortgage lending and retail deposits, nor the associated vagaries in the relationship between £M3, which includes bank deposits, and PSL2 which also includes deposits with building societies (whose bank deposits are excluded) (see the Loughborough lecture by the Governor of the Bank of England, Robin Leigh-Pemberton (1986). What I want to do is to discuss the response of the personal sector to the new opportunities created by this set of developments. I shall also argue that the process of 'liberalisation' is not complete and that its completion might actually involve the reversal of recent trends in the scale of intermediation with the personal sector.

7.3 HOUSE PRICES AND PORTFOLIO ADJUSTMENT

The personal sector's reaction to its new flexibility in borrowing cannot be divorced from the initial situation created by the interaction of general inflation and, in particular, rising house prices, with the previous restrictions. The obstacles to increasing mortgage borrowing meant that rising house prices and unindexed mortgages raised the proportion of housing 'equity' in persons' portfolios. The reduction of these obstacles has left people freer to restructure their portfolios as they choose. In practice this has meant additional borrowing to acquire other assets whether consumer durables, corporate securities or liquid assets.[1]

It is in some respects misleading to refer to the difference between the value of one's house and of one's mortgage as one's equity in the house. From a portfolio theory viewpoint the homeowner's exposure to house price fluctuations is proportional to the value of the house unadjusted for the mortgage. Even if the house's value falls below that of the mortgage the borrower's liability is not limited to that value. Only bankruptcy puts a lower limit to the exposure, but this is no different from any other risk that is run. Thus there is little more reason to regard the excess of the value of the house over the mortgage as 'equity' than to regard one's equity in other assets as being reduced by pledging them as collateral.

For this reason I think it better to look at the portfolio adjustment as being a response to the increase in wealth generated by what were in effect forced savings resulting from rising house prices and eroding real debt. This increases demand for other assets *and* supply of liabilities; it is the relatively low cost of mortgage credit that makes it the preferred liability to issue in this restructuring process.

What assets have been acquired in the process? It is difficult to relate changes in the personal sector's balance sheet directly to the changes in access to credit and terms of deposits described in Section 7.2 and even more difficult to trace it through to individuals whose circumstances and reactions may differ widely. It appears, however, that the greater part has gone on financial assets, mostly liquid, and on consumer durables (including cars). In a sectorally closed system additional deposits by households wishing to hold more of their wealth in that form would be the only source of funds for additional mortgage lending. In practice it will have been possible for households to extract cash to purchase durables to the extent that mortgages were financed by funds other than household deposits.

Despite the sale of public sector assets through privatisations household sector *acquisition* of corporate securities has in fact continued to be negative. This is, of course, not true of the life assurance and pension funds who have large and growing holdings of these securities for the benefit of households. The movement of relatively available mortgage debt towards the role of marginal source of credit while high return accounts have been introduced (despite the waning of inflation) means that the cost of financing liquid asset positions by borrowing has fallen markedly.

From this point of view it may not be surprising that the personal sector has expanded both sides of its balance sheet from £450 billion and 55 per cent of personal disposable income at the end of 1980 to £550 billion and 80 per cent respectively in 1986. If we restrict consideration to financial assets and liabilities the figures are £175 billion and 55 per cent at the end of 1980 and £275 billion and 85 per cent respectively in mid 1986. In these latter terms it is striking that both increases are the same proportion of the initial stock.

It is also true, as Sprenkle and Miller (1980) have argued, that as the spread between borrowing and lending rates goes to zero so the demand for such liquidity may become unbounded. It is demanded, however, principally to ensure the availability of funds when they are needed. Sufficient confidence in access to credit makes such liquidity redundant. Moreover, however narrow the interest rate spread, the tax on deposit interest, even at the reduced CRT rate, while debt interest is not generally tax deductible, makes carrying borrowed liquidity expensive.

For this reason one might question whether any householder does indeed normally carry very much of it. Certainly one can foresee institutional developments which would ensure that he did not. This would be what might be called a 'home equity account'. This would be a very simple combination of a mortgage with an overdraft facility. On the basis of the applicant's income, and the value of his house, a credit limit would be set which might well be linked, at least partially, to general indices of earnings and house prices. Repayment schedules might be fixed by agreement with an easy arrangement for borrowing to narrow any gap between the actual debt and the credit ceiling. Such a scheme would also meet one of the points made a few years ago when the possibility of indexed mortgages was raised. It was then said that many couples actually welcomed the front end loading of unindexed mortgages which brought the heaviest real outgoings into phase with the period in which both husband and wife were working full time. With computerised record keeping there is no reason why an account with a credit ceiling secured on one's house should not, like a credit card account, require a minimum repayment and indicate the current level of the credit ceiling while allowing more rapid repayments as desired. Given confidence in the continuation of such arrangements it would be irrational for anyone borrowing in this way from an institution offering chequing facilities to have any funds on deposit at all.

Thus the continuation of current trends in access to credit will have two possibly countervailing effects. While intermediation between surplus and deficit units should continue to grow with a reduction in its costs, the growth of credit and deposits relative to income and wealth may well be curbed by the elimination of borrowing by units in overall surplus and deposits by units in overall deficit.

7.4 POLICY IMPLICATIONS

In this section I want to address the questions of how the effects and effectiveness of monetary policy might be changed by the liberalisation of financial markets taken together with the development and spread of hedging instruments and techniques.

For much of the post-war period in many industrial countries the effect of monetary policy, even when not explicitly in terms of credit quotas or controls on hire-purchase terms, depended on interaction with interest rate ceilings and other administrative controls now largely abandoned. Suppose therefore that most agents have relatively free access to credit. There will, of course, always be people who feel rationed because others do not share their enthusiasm for the prospects of their career or their project (see Stiglitz and Weiss, 1981; Jaffee and Russell, 1976). Suppose also that they are free to borrow directly, or indirectly through swaps, at the maturity and in the currency of their choice. What then will happen if the authorities vary short-term interest rates in pursuit of the objectives of monetary policy?

In the past interest rate rises in both the US and UK impinged particularly on the domestic housing market, through availability and rationing effects, and on other sectors through the exchange rate. The first of these effects may have disappeared with the end of interest ceilings and rationing. Does the second disappear if international traders have hedged their position in the financial market?

What I have in mind here goes further than merely covering foreign exchange positions contract by contract. That has nearly always been possible, though not always done, and has the effect that many things people want to explain by reference to the spot exchange rate are probably better explained by reference to the three-month rate. More recently, however, a London based consulting service selling mainly in dollars to US clients might have decided that it expected to earn $1 million a year in that way for the next few years and, having sterling salary costs, decided to sell forward dollars for sterling for two or three years ahead even though it had no firm contracts beyond the end of the current year.

Taken to an extreme, which is probably not yet practicable, a corporation deciding where to put a manufacturing plant to supply the world market, and realising its vulnerability to real exchange-rate movements, would hedge currency, and relative unit labour cost, movements over the 20-year life of the plant. Does such behaviour make monetary policy ineffective?

Let us take these cases in turn after making some general points. Clearly hedging against the risk of short-term interest rate changes makes it possible for those who have hedged to ignore them. If I have a 20-year fixed rate mortgage short-term swings in the rate have no direct impact and I need not revise any of my plans. It may however continue to have income – or rather wealth – effects, if the 20-year mortgage rate rises; I could, in principle, buy back my debt for less than its face value. Probably more relevantly, the timing of my general consumption expenditures should reflect the changed intertemporal relative prices. This should reduce expenditure and raise cash-flow savings as there is no offset from increased interest outgoings.

Whether the impact of a given change in interest rates on expenditures is as large as under the old system remains an empirical question, but even if it were smaller there could well be large welfare gains as the old system left some people in extremely vulnerable positions; unhedged and without rights of access to additional finance even to relieve extreme distress. How completely hedged is it feasible for people to be? Who if anyone will hold short-term assets and liabilities?

I have argued elsewhere (Flemming, 1989) that if people held wealth as a hedge against future consumption requirements in a life-cycle framework there would, if the (indexed) yield curve were contingently flat, be considerable demand for short-term assets – more than for any other maturity. Even if this were not true, and all government debt were perpetual, a short rate would still exist and be relevant to short-term intertemporal planning.

Turning to the exchange rate effects of monetary policy a somewhat similar situation arises. The income, or wealth, effect of exchange rate changes are largely offset. My London based consultancy becomes less competitive, its operations less profitable, if the dollar falls, but its owners are compensated by a profit on their forward sale of dollars. It is thus open to the enterprise to use those profits to subsidise operating losses – but it would make more profit by cutting back its operation to the extent that the sterling income demands of its employees cease to be compatible with the willingness to pay of its dollar customers. Similarly with the factory, it may pay to use it less intensively than had been planned, but there need be no hole in the company's balance sheet even if it is closed – or mothballed.

The rising DM in a hedged world would still make Germany a less profitable place in which to produce but it would not necessarily reduce the value of German enterprises. This means that while output, and perhaps income, fall there need not necessarily be a further reduction in demand on account of capital losses. Of course if the shares of the enterprise were held in a sufficiently globally diversified portfolio there might be no presumption that they were held by nationals anyway. Indeed sufficient global diversification might make explicit hedging unnecessary, but this is unlikely as principal/agent problems make it optimal for founders or managers of firms to be required to hold stakes in them that exceed what they would ideally choose to hold in a diversified portfolio. These agents will then have an incentive either to hedge their own holdings or to undertake hedging strategies within the firm which reduce the fluctuation in the value of their asset.

7.5 CONCLUSION

There have been significant innovations in both the domestic retail deposit and credit markets, and their linkage to global markets. These have the effect of narrowing the gap between the world we live in and that inhabited by text book writers. As one of the latter, albeit responsible for advising a monetary authority, I can see the welfare advantages of these developments more clearly than any cost in terms of lost control. I should, perhaps, nevertheless, say that like many others I am uneasy about the level of resources, particularly of human capital, that the new markets seem liable to absorb (cf. Tobin, 1984).

Note

1. Since this paper was presented in 1987, the sharp rise in house prices has been reversed with the first signs of a revival of the housing market not appearing until the Spring of 1991. [Editor.]

References

Flemming, J. S. (1989) 'Three Points on the Yield Curve' in A. S. Courakis and C. A. E. Goodhart (eds), *The Monetary Economics of John Hicks* (London: Macmillan).

Jaffee, D. M. and Russell, T. (1976) 'Imperfect Information, Uncertainty and Credit Rationing', *Quarterly Journal of Economics*, 90, 4, November, pp. 651–66.

Leigh-Pemberton, R. (1986) 'Financial Change and Broad Money', *Bank of England Quarterly Bulletin*, 26, 4, December, pp. 499–507 (Loughborough University Banking Centre Annual Lecture in Finance delivered by the Governor of the Bank of England on 22 October 1986.

Sprenkle, C. M. and Miller, M. H. (1980) 'The Precautionary Demand for Narrow and Broad Money', *Economica*, 47, 188, November, pp. 407–21.

Stiglitz, J. E. and Weiss, A. (1981) 'Credit Rationing in Markets with Imperfect Information', *American Economic Review*, 71, 3, June, pp. 393–410.

Tobin, J. (1984) 'On the Efficiency of the Financial System', *Lloyds Bank Review*, 153, July, pp. 1–15 (Fred Hirsch Memorial Lecture given in New York on 15 May 1984).

8 Capital Flows and Exchange Rates: Some Implications*

Gordon T. Pepper

8.1 INTRODUCTION

Much innovation in the financial field has been based on the revolution in information and communications technology. One of the most dramatic developments has been the globalisation of securities markets, which happened very suddenly.

Flows of long-term capital across exchanges have grown in size, to such an extent that they can now be more important than flows of short-term capital or imbalances on current accounts of balance of payments. Flows of long-term capital that are dominant and persist have important implications. This chapter discusses some of them.

8.2 THE DRIVING FORCE BEHIND EXCHANGE RATES

The balance of payments has four components: (i) current account, (ii) short-term capital account, (iii) long-term capital account and (iv) official intervention. The current account used to be the driving force behind movements in exchange rates. If the current account was moving into greater deficit, a currency tended to weaken, and vice versa if there was a growing surplus. The authorities reacted to pressure on the exchange rate by intervening in the foreign exchange market, by changing interest rates or by deflating the economy in other ways. In the 1950s and 1960s exchange rates were fixed under the Bretton Woods agreement and exchange controls limited capital flows. The result was that changes in the current account dominated the balance of payments, with official intervention the main offsetting component.

In the late 1960s and early 1970s speculative transactions grew in importance. The eurocurrency markets grew greatly in size, the forward foreign exchange market developed and the capacity of the spot market increased substantially. Speculative transactions were sufficiently large to force parity changes and speculators were greatly encouraged by the profits which were made over devaluations. These speculative transactions were based initially on expectations of current accounts and subsequently on the way the authorities would react to the resulting foreign exchange pressure. The causal sequence of events ran from current accounts to other factors.

In the 1970s short-term capital flows not only continued to grow in size but also started to become independent of the behaviour of current accounts. A good example of this was UK experience in 1974. Because of a huge rise in the price of oil and overheating of the domestic economy, there was a deterioration in the current account of the UK's balance of payments which was very dramatic by the standards of the time. There were, accordingly, widespread forecasts that sterling would decline in value. Much to many people's surprise, sterling stayed firm for many months. The explanation was a large inflow of short-term capital, in spite of most speculators being bearish. This was the result of a vicious monetary squeeze, the effects of which will be discussed later. The important point at this stage of the discussion is that it happened. A capital flow was greater than a major current account imbalance, largely independent of the current account and in the opposite direction to the current imbalance, in the sense that its effect on the exchange rate was in the opposite direction to that of the current account.

In the 1980s long-term capital movements in turn rose greatly in size, as a result of the revolution in information and communication technology, financial innovation, the dismantling of controls and the globalisation of securities markets. Further, flows of long-term capital are likely to be even more independent of current accounts than short-term capital movements. US experience in 1984 illustrates the extent to which capital flows can now be both larger than a major current account imbalance and move in the opposite direction.

During the 1980s speculators learnt that there can be quite prolonged periods when current accounts of balance of payments are clearly not the underlying causal force behind exchange rate movements. Speculators are, accordingly, now much less likely to base transactions on expectations of current accounts (see Appendix 8.1). This weakens the influence of current accounts on exchange rates still further.[1]

8.3 GROWING CURRENT ACCOUNT IMBALANCES

The importance of the direction as well as the size of a capital flow should be stressed at an early stage. If a capital flow is in the same direction as a current account imbalance (note this can only happen if the central bank is intervening) the exchange rate will tend to move in the 'right direction', in the sense that the movement will in due course help to restore the current account to balance. Suppose, for example, that the current account is in deficit. A fall in the exchange rate will discourage imports and encourage exports; after an initial 'J' effect from the deterioration in the terms of trade, the current account deficit will tend to reduce. Further, the reaction of the authorities to a weak currency will have a similar effect. Any rise in interest rates or other deflationary measures will depress the domestic economy and this will reduce the demand for imports and free productive capacity for exports. Any intervention in the foreign exchange market to support the currency will also tend to deflate the economy, because it will have a contractionary impact on the money supply (unless it is completely sterilised).

In the opposite case of a capital flow in the opposite direction to a current account imbalance, the outcome will be very different if the capital flow is the larger. The exchange rate will then move in the 'wrong' direction. *The imbalance on the current account will tend to become progressively greater as long as the capital flow is dominant and does not change direction.*[2] If the current account imbalance is a deficit, the process may continue until the size of the deficit reaches such proportions that there is a crisis of confidence. The capital flow then will suddenly reverse; it will change to the same direction as the current imbalance and the exchange rate will fall dramatically.

8.4 FOREIGN EXCHANGE INTERVENTION

In a world in which capital flows can be dominant and largely independent of current accounts, exchange rates will swing wildly over the medium term. One consequence of this is the massive intervention by central banks in foreign exchange markets in attempts to stop rates moving in the 'wrong' direction. The monetary effects of such intervention will subsequently be a major factor affecting the global cycle. This important subject is discussed in Appendix 8.2.[3]

8.5 GLOBAL BUSINESS CYCLE

Capital flows dominating exchange rates have other important implications for the global business cycle. If current accounts are dominant, powerful forces will be at work deflating countries with balance of payments deficits and stimulating countries with balance of payments surpluses, as explained. *The result will be that the business cycles of different countries will tend to be out of step.* If one country is enjoying an expansion whilst another is suffering a contraction, the sum of activity in both countries may not alter. If the business cycles of different countries are out of step, the global business cycle will be muted. *If capital flows are dominant and in the opposite direction to current account imbalances, countries will not be pushed out of step with each other and the global cycle will not be muted.*

8.6 CAPITAL FLOWS: THE PRICE MECHANISM

As the implications of the capital flows are very important for exchange rates, current account imbalances and business cycles, it is very important to understand why movements of capital occur. Capital will flow from one country to another either as a result of the price mechanism or because of supply/demand pressures. Dealing first with the former, capital will flow into a country if foreigners expect the rate of return to be higher than that in their own and other countries. The return has two components: the expected return in local currency terms and the expected change in foreign exchange rate.

The most important explanation for a high nominal rate of return in local currency terms is usually high price inflation. Whereas foreign investors should deduct the expected fall in the foreign exchange rate from the return in nominal terms, domestic investors deduct the expected decline in the domestic purchasing power of the currency, that is, the expected rate of inflation. In the short run the two deductions can be very different, especially if current accounts are not dominating exchange rates. Current account imbalances cannot, however, last for ever and the two are connected in the long run via purchasing power parities for internationally traded goods.

While the difference between the two deductions should be remembered, a useful starting-point for analysis is the expected real return in local currency terms. One reason for this is that the returns available in a country are determined initially by factors domestic to its economy. Foreigners tend initially to be 'price takers'. The prices set by domestic factors then adjust as a result of the foreign transactions. As domestic factors precede external ones it is logical to start with the former.

High real rates of return in a country can be a sign of either a healthy or an unhealthy economy. They will be a sign of health if the real rate of return on capital employed is higher than that in other countries. They will be a sign of malaise if high real rates are needed to combat permissive fiscal policy, low personal savings (for example, because consumers have an excessive propensity to borrow) or a weak currency.[4]

8.7 THE HEALTHY CASE

Starting with the healthy case, a country which is enjoying a rate of return on capital employed higher than the average abroad (for example, on industrial investment, because of innovation, efficient management, low wage costs, etc.) will experience an inflow of long-term capital and its exchange rate will tend to rise. The current account of its balance of payments will then tend to move into deficit. The inflow of capital will be the cause of the deficit.

Although the country is borrowing from abroad, it will be using the funds to accumulate productive assets at home. This is how developed countries have historically financed developing countries, especially those with abundant natural resources. The process is highly desirable in terms of global economic efficiency. Capital is a scarce resource and it should flow into the countries where it can be used most efficiently. Moves of current accounts into deficit for this reason are not a cause for concern. Foreigners are unlikely to lose confidence in the currencies of successful countries.

8.8 SIGN OF MALAISE

High real rates which are a sign of malaise are a different matter altogether. Suppose, for example, that fiscal policy has been eased substantially. If a rise in inflation is to be avoided, the increase in the budget deficit must not be financed by the government printing money, that is, by borrowing from banks. It should be financed by an increase in genuine savings. The yields on government bonds will rise to encourage this to happen. The level of domestic savings may, however, be slow to respond. With bond markets having become global, the rise in yields may easily attract foreign investors before domestic investors have increased their savings sufficiently.

It should be noted that foreigners need merely to exchange one investment for another – an investment in one currency for an investment in another – whereas the need domestically is for an increase in the aggregate of private savings. The former can take place more quickly than the latter.

If bond yields respond quickly to the rise in the budget deficit, a capital inflow from abroad will tend to precede a move towards deficit in the current account of the balance of payments, because of the boost to domestic demand from the easing of fiscal policy. The exchange rate will rise, and this will then increase the current account deficit further.

The point about the foreign reaction materialising more quickly than the required domestic response is very important. If a domestic investor switches one investment for another, for example if he sells an ordinary share and buys a gilt-edged stock, the total of private net savings does not alter. The response of total savings to a rise in the real rate of interest is complex and can be slow to materialise. *A securities transaction can take place much more quickly than macro-economic aggregates alter.*[5]

The position is similar if personal savings suddenly fall. The most likely reason for this will be a rise in borrowing by consumers. The rise in borrowing will tend to increase the rate of growth of the money supply. Interest rates will then need to rise if an increase in inflation is to be avoided. (Under some countries' mechanism of monetary control, the rise in interest rates to stop the growth of the money supply from increasing will be automatic.) The rise in rates may well attract foreign investors before it succeeds in boosting private net savings, in particular before it discourages consumer borrowing. The response of consumer borrowing to a rise in interest rates is only rapid if rates are increased to a crisis level and there is a major shock to confidence.

If high real rates are due to permissive fiscal policy or a consumer spending spree, the inflow of capital, that is, the borrowing from abroad, will not be matched by an increase in productive assets. The inflow allows the government or consumer to escape discipline for a while. Remedial measures can be postponed. Eventually they will have to be taken and when the 'stop' comes it is likely to be more drastic.

The effect of capital inflows on domestic demand and GDP in the shorter run, that is, before the stop occurs, was mentioned earlier. A deficit country is not forced to deflate. Domestic demand can continue to accelerate. The business cycle will not break step with that in the rest of the world. Further, reduced exports and increased imports will marginally stimulate economic activity in other countries. The global business cycle will not be muted but, if anything, will be accentuated.[6]

8.9 EXPECTATIONS OF CAPITAL PROFIT

Moving on with the analysis, an inflow of capital can occur because of expectations of capital profit in the relatively short run rather than as a result of high current income. Cyclical changes in the level of the bond and stockmarkets associated with the business cycle are well known phenomena. Consider a country in which the domestic business cycle is tending to be in advance of that of the rest of the world. Suppose that economic growth is tending downwards whilst the rest of the world is still expanding. Classic conditions will exist for the start of a bull market in bonds in the country tending downwards, whereas bond markets in the rest of the world will continue to be in a bear phase. International bond funds will then pour into the country tending downwards, as happened in the US in July 1989. The money flowing into the country will tend to postpone its economic downturn (as interest rates fall and the money supply is boosted). The flows of bond capital will tend to push the country back into step with the rest of the world.

8.10 CAPITAL FLOWS: PRESSURE OF SUPPLY AND DEMAND

It was stated earlier that capital flows can occur either as a result of the price mechanism or because of supply/demand pressures. There is, for example, no reason why countries should have the same propensity to save. Some, for example Japan, may have chronic surplus savings. They may, for instance, have an ageing population and people may wish to provide for their old age. Others, for

example the US, may have low savings. Long-term capital will flow
from countries with surplus savings to those with a shortage.

In countries with a surplus, people will initially tend to invest at
home. Asset prices will rise and, as this happens, the real return on
capital will fall. The opposite will tend to occur in countries with a
shortage; asset prices will fall and the real return on capital will rise.
The price mechanism will encourage capital to flow from surplus to
deficit countries. This is part of a normal process of economic
adjustment and is not a cause for concern. (The optimum strategy for
portfolio managers is interesting. While asset prices are adjusting,
the best tactic is to invest in the country with surplus savings in order
to benefit from the rise in prices. Once the adjustment is over, funds
should be switched into the country with low savings as the return on
capital will be greater.)

8.11 MONETARY GROWTH

Another form of supply/demand pressure, especially important for
short-term capital flows, is relative monetary growth. If one country
has easy money and another has a monetary squeeze, money will
tend to flow from the former to the latter. Similarly, if one country
has an abundant supply of credit and another has a credit squeeze,
funds will tend to flow from the first to the second country. (The
monetary and credit pressures will normally be in the same direction
but this is not necessarily so under some countries' method of control
over their banking system.) Such flows of capital tend to relieve
monetary squeezes and mop up surpluses relative to the average of
other countries. Accordingly, they tend to reduce an important force
pushing the business cycles of different countries out of step.

Some people may argue that there is no difference between the
price mechanism and supply/demand pressures. The two are, indeed,
closely related, as has been described. Monetary pressure does,
however, provide an important insight into when a change in interest
rates is becoming effective. The earlier discussion was in terms of the
level of interest rates in real terms, that is, the level in nominal terms
less the expected rate of inflation. It is important to distinguish
between this and rates which are high in nominal terms relative to the
current rate of inflation. The behaviour of the money supply assists
greatly in making the distinction. Expressed in another way, there
are many occasions when an exchange rate does not respond to a rise

in interest rates. This is likely to be so as long as monetary growth remains excessive. If the rise in rates is sufficient to curb excessive monetary growth, the exchange rate is also likely to respond.[7]

8.12 SUMMARY

The change during the 1970s and the 1980s has not been merely first short-term capital flows and then long-term capital flows growing in size relative to the current account of the balance of payments. Capital flows used to be based mainly on expectations of the current account (and of official reaction). The more important change is that capital flows may now be independent of the current account.

The fact of capital flows rather than current accounts driving exchange rates is responsible for rates moving in the 'wrong' direction, trade imbalances tending to persist or growing progressively greater and central banks intervening massively in the foreign exchange markets. The last can have important implications for the global business cycle.

A capital inflow can be a sign either of a healthy economy or of economic malaise. In the former case, high real rates of return on industrial investment and so on will attract foreign investment. In the latter case, foreigners will be attracted by the high rates of interest which are needed to combat permissive fiscal policy or a consumer spending spree.

Foreigners can execute securities transactions much more quickly than a domestic macroeconomic aggregate can alter. If bond yields rise by more than any increase in inflationary expectations, a capital inflow from abroad may well precede a rise in net domestic savings; that is, the capital inflow will precede a move towards deficit in the current account of the balance of payments.

As well as the price mechanism, supply and demand pressures are an important determinant of capital flows. Examples of this are demographic factors and relative monetary and credit pressures.

If current accounts are driving exchange rates, countries in deficit have to deflate, their business cycles are pushed out of step with the rest of the world and this tends to mute the global cycle. When capital accounts drive exchange rates this process does not occur; indeed countries tend to be pushed into step with each other. The global cycle could therefore be accentuated.

If one country has chronic surplus savings and another has a chronic deficiency, the optimum strategy for portfolio managers is to invest in the former country while real rates of return on capital are adjusting and in the latter after they have adjusted.

In the foreign exchange market, people no longer know whether economic news is good or bad for a currency. A very important cause of market fluctuations has disappeared, exposing the ebb and flow of underlying business, technical factors and the herd instinct (Appendix 8.1).

The effect of a budget deficit on a domestic economy depends on whether it is financed by borrowing from banks or from non-banks. Similarly, the effect of the US trade deficit on other countries depends on whether it is financed by central banks or other sources (Appendix 8.2).

Appendix 8.1 Market Fluctuations and Economic News

When current accounts were the driving force behind exchange rate movements, market participants could judge whether news about the economy was good or bad for the exchange rate. Now that either current accounts or capital flows may be the driving force, the position is confused. This is especially so when many people do not understand the determinants of the capital flows. The result is that they may not be able to judge whether a particular news item should be good or bad for the exchange rate.

Contrast the above with the position in the gilt-edged market. News of a rise in inflationary pressure is clearly bearish; news of waning inflationary pressure is bullish. News of economic growth at an unsustainable rate is bearish, news of recessionary tendency is bullish. News of a weak currency is bearish; that of a strong currency is bullish. Because the direction of the impact on the gilt-edged market is known, prices react to such news announcements. Even if no transactions take place, market makers will adjust prices in the appropriate direction. As such items of news occur regularly, market prices will be adjusted frequently. As many of the economic series are erratic, gilt-edged prices will fluctuate accordingly.

Returning to the foreign exchange market, news that an economy is slowing down may be good or bad for an exchange rate. On the one hand, the balance of trade will tend to improve. On the other, interest rates may be reduced and short-term capital may flow out as a result. The slowdown may also discourage both direct investment and portfolio investment in equities by foreigners, or it may encourage non-residents to invest in bonds. Further, the slowdown may be a symptom and, therefore, confirmation of a financial squeeze, the continuing effect of which will be to strengthen the currency. The balance of such forces is unclear. There are many occasions when people simply do not know what the effect on the exchange rate of an item of news should be. If it is unclear what the effect should be, the foreign exchange market will not react to economic news and an important cause of frequent fluctuations will disappear.

In the absence of fluctuations caused by economic news, the market will tend to be driven by the ebb and flow of underlying business, for example commercial orders. Speculation will be based on this rather than on economic news. The technical situation will also be important; the market may be 'over-bought' or 'under-bought'; that is, speculators may be fully committed or out of the market. In such circumstances, fundamental analysis will be neglected, because the influence of the fundamentals is unclear even if they can be analysed correctly. In contrast, technical analysis (chartism) will be popular. Further, market participants will observe the type of code of conduct which appears to be successful. In particular, if following trends leads to success, the herd instinct will be dominant.

Appendix 8.2 Central Bank Intervention and the Global Business Cycle

The impact of the US trade deficit on the rest of the world in the 1980s was similar to that of a budget deficit on an individual country.

8.2.1 A budget deficit in an individual country

Keynesians argue that an increase in a budget deficit will boost demand in the country concerned and that this will lead to a rise in its GDP (they also argue that real activity rather than inflation will increase providing the level of demand is not excessive). Monetarists argue that the effect of an increase in a budget deficit on GDP depends on how it is financed. If it is financed by government borrowing from banks, that is, by printing money, they agree with Keynesians that GDP will rise (but they argue that price inflation rather than real activity will increase in the longer term). If the budget deficit is financed by borrowing from non-banks, that is, by genuine savings, Monetarists disagree with Keynesians; they argue that there will be very little, if any, effect on GDP because the money supply will not alter. In Keynesian language, they argue that a rise in savings will offset the stimulus to demand from the increase in the budget deficit.

8.2.2 US trade deficit and the rest of the world

There is a similar argument that the impact of a US trade deficit on the rest of the world also depends on how it is financed. If there are no offsetting factors a rise in the US trade deficit will stimulate production in the rest of the world, as countries' net exports to the US rise. The US trade deficit can be financed either by a capital inflow or by central bank intervention in foreign exchange markets. It can be argued that the former is similar to a budget deficit being financed by borrowing from non-banks, whereas the latter is similar to it being financed by banks.

If the US trade deficit is financed by a capital inflow, the US syphons off other countries' savings and this neutralises the boost to demand in the rest

Table 8A.1 Impact of a rise in the US budget and trade deficit

	Effects on GNP	
	In the US	In the rest of the world
Domestic Borrowing		
Case 1 from non-banks	Nil	Nil
Case 2 from banks	Stimulation	Nil
Foreign Borrowing		
Case 3 capital inflow	Nil	Nil
Case 4 central bank intervention	Nil	Stimulation

of the world from the US trade deficit; economic activity in the rest of the world should not therefore be affected. If the US trade deficit is financed by central bank intervention, other countries' savings are not syphoned off and the boost to demand in the rest of the world from the US trade deficit is not neutralised. Expressed in monetarist language, a country's money supply is increased if either its central bank intervenes to resist a rise in its currency or the Fed intervenes in the country's currency to resist a fall in the dollar (assuming the intervention is not deliberately 'sterilised'). If central banks do not intervene the money supply in other countries is not affected. Put in yet another way, the central bank intervention allows an outflow of dollars as a result of a US trade deficit to enter the domestic monetary systems of other countries. A classic example of this was the intervention in 1987 under the Louvre Accord which liquefied non-US OECD economies and marked the start of the rapid economic expansion in the rest of the world.

8.2.3 US trade deficit and activity in the US

A rise in the US trade deficit reduces activity within the US, as domestic demand is met by a rise in goods imported from abroad and as US exports fall.

8.2.4 A rise in the US budget deficit and subsequently in the trade deficit

Table 8A.1 summarises the effects on GNP in both the US and the rest of the world of, initially, a rise in the US budget deficit and, subsequently, a move into deficit of the balance of trade. There are four cases.

Case 1 The trade deficit has not yet risen and the increase in the US budget deficit is financed domestically by the government borrowing from outside the banking system. This is the domestic 'crowding out' scenario. There is no effect on GNP, in either the US or the rest of the world.

Case 2 The trade deficit has still not risen but the increase in the US budget deficit is financed domestically by the government borrowing from banks. This is the classic example of stimulation of domestic demand.

In the next two cases the trade deficit has risen in response to the US budget deficit; that is, the increase in the budget deficit is financed by foreign rather than domestic borrowing.

Case 3 The rise in the trade deficit is financed by a capital inflow. Domestically within the US, the stimulus from the budget deficit is neutralised by the rise in the trade deficit. Externally, the boost to activity in other countries from the trade deficit is offset by savings being syphoned off by the US.

Case 4 The rise in the trade deficit is financed by central bank intervention. Economic activity in the rest of the world is stimulated because the offset has disappeared. The US budget deficit is, in effect, liquefying other countries' economies rather than that of the US.

Notes and References

* The author is in the debt of Alec Chrystal and Geoffrey Wood for helpful comments and discussion; any errors, of course, remain the author's.

1. For further discussion see W. M. Corden (1985) *Inflation, Exchange Rates and the World Economy: Lectures on International Monetary Economics*, 3rd ed. (Oxford: Clarendon Press). Modern exchange rate theory starts from the proposition that exchange rates are determined in asset markets. See, for example, R. MacDonald (1988) *Floating Exchange Rates: Theories & Evidence* (London: Unwin Hyman); D. Begg (1989) 'Floating Exchange Rates in Theory and Practice', *Oxford Review of Economic Policy*, 5, no. 3, Autumn, pp. 24–39.
2. For an analysis of the wealth effects associated with cumulative current account imbalances see R. Dornbusch and S. Fischer (1980) 'Exchange rates and the Current Account', *American Economic Review*, 70, no. 5, December, pp. 960–71.
3. A possible mechanism for this is suggested by McKinnon: R. I. McKinnon (1982) 'Currency Substitution and Instability in the World Dollar Market', *American Economic Review*, 72, no. 3, June, pp. 320–33. For further discussion see D. V. Coes (1987) 'Exchange Rate Intervention and Imperfect Capital Mobility' in D. R. Hodgman and G. E. Wood (eds.), *Monetary and Exchange Rate Policy* (London: Macmillan).
4. See K. A. Chrystal and G. E. Wood (1988) 'Are Trade Deficits a Problem?', *Federal Reserve Bank of St. Louis Review*, 70, no. 1, Jan/Feb, pp. 3–11.
5. This fact is central to the entire class of 'overshooting' models. See R. Dornbusch (1976) 'Expectations and Exchange Rate Dynamics', *Journal of Political Economy*, 84, no. 6, December, pp. 1161–76.
6. P. R. Krugman (1989) *Exchange Rate Instability* (Cambridge, Mass: MIT Press).
7. Empirically the nominal rate and inflation expectations effects can be separated; see J. A. Frenkel (1979) 'On the Mark: A Theory of Floating Exchange Rates Based on Real Interest Differentials', *American Economic Review*, 69, no. 4, September, pp. 610–27.

9 British Monetary Policy: October 1990

C. A. E. Goodhart

9.1 INTRODUCTION

It is, I would claim, desirable for the authorities to have a coherent strategy for the conduct of monetary policy. By coherent strategy I do not necessarily mean hard and fast rules, but certainly a strategy. When one is charged with the conduct of monetary policy, it helps if you can rationalise what you are doing, first of all to yourself, and after that to others in the general public. If there is such a strategy that can be outlined, it is likely that policy itself will be more consistent; that there will be less misinterpretation of what policy measures might imply; and a greater stabilisation of expectations. It is arguable that there was not any such (publicly expressed) strategy in the monetary field between 1985, when the then Chancellor Lawson threw over the broad £M3 target and the end of 1990 when Chancellor Lamont expressed firm adherence to maintaining the parity of £ within the Exchange Rate Mechanism (ERM) of the European Monetary System (EMS).

The only previous time when there did appear, to outsiders, to be a strategy (though one which was never publicly expressed and always remained somewhat obscure) was the period from March 1987 till March 1988, when we were apparently shadowing the Deutsche Mark (DM). We behaved then for a time as if we were giving the European Exchange Rate Mechanism a trial run, which, as will be remembered, ended in dissension and disputes in the Spring of 1988. Then there was a period when the interest rate was changed in a way that, given the otherwise determined changes in the exchange rate, would seem to be such as to bring about a given level of nominal incomes, along the lines of the Treasury internal model, but that, in turn, broke down in the face of worsening inflation in the latter part of 1988.

In the first two years after 1985, when we no longer had a clear monetary strategy, its absence did not seem to matter all that much, because economic developments then were highly favourable; they must have been about the two best years for the British economy on record. Unfortunately, since then, economic developments have become much less favourable, and inflation re-accelerated. So, it had become less acceptable to allow the authorities the discretion to fly by the seat of their pants, since we may ask why we should continue to trust those whose discretion has apparently got us into our present unpleasant conjuncture. Given the undesirability of just continuing in that discretionary fashion, I now want to consider a number of possible alternative strategies.

The first alternative that one might have considered would be to revert to a revised, or adjusted, form of monetary targetry. Indeed we have had *some* monetary targetry ever since 1985, in the form of M0, though this, I believe, has mainly represented a fig leaf to disguise the actual fact of the abandonment of monetary targetry, a fig leaf that enables the Chancellor to say that he never gave up monetary targetry. Since 1985, however, I have failed to discern any single case when the monetary authorities took a monetary policy step, such as changing interest rates, which depended primarily on the movements of M0. There have been a number of policy measures in which the development of M0 has been called in aid as one of the contributory factors, but it has usually been the exchange rate, or inflation, or some such other development, rather than M0 itself, that has brought about the policy instrument shift. Given the fact that M0 is widely regarded as no more than a somewhat noisy current and/or possibly short leading indicator of present developments in nominal current expenditures, (particularly consumer expenditures), it would be hard to persuade anyone in the City, or elsewhere, to take M0 much more seriously, even if the authorities were inclined in that direction.

There have also been suggestions by some economists, such as McCallum, Meltzer and Poole, (see, for example, McCallum (1987 and 1988)), to revert to a monetary target for, say, US M1, or in the UK for one of the broad monetary aggregates, even though velocity remains somewhat unpredictable. McCallum's proposals depend on the proposition that, although you may not be able to predict velocity very well over a run of future years, at least you can hope that it will not usually change very much, or jump far, from where it has been in the recent past. So you may assume that velocity is some weighted average of its current and recent past levels in setting the monetary target. If we had, indeed, begun on that basis in 1979–80 with a monetary target based on a velocity estimate which was assumed to be uncertain and unreliable (and thus with a numerical target which was expressly revised each year), it might have made the conduct of monetary targetry in those earlier years possibly somewhat better. At least it would have been appreciated that the underlying relationships on which the monetary targets were based were more variable than was asserted in the original Medium-Term Financial Strategy (MTFS). But now, given the history that we have had in the UK (and what has happened to monetary targetry in a range of other countries such as the USA) and the uncertainty about the movements in velocity, together with some further doubts about the control methods involved, the suggestion that we should revert to monetary targets at this juncture is simply not feasible. It would not be credible; it would not achieve the public support and belief that is needed.

9.2   A NOMINAL INCOME TARGET?

In any case the whole idea of monetary targetry was to try to achieve desirable outcomes for nominal incomes, for prices and real output. Let us, once again, revert to that standard, splendid identity, $MV = PY$ where M = money stock, V = income velocity of circulation, P = price level, Y = income, and note that if V is now regarded as so volatile and unpredictable, as to make it no longer worthwhile considering broader (or narrower) monetary aggregate targets, (since one does not know what V is going to be), why not just have a target which relates policy instruments directly to the developments either of nominal incomes, or of the movement of prices (inflation) in isolation. While nominal income targets have many attractions in *principle*, the practicalities of trying to base policy on statistics which are always delayed (and when they actually come out frequently point in differing directions owing to statistical error) are much more daunting. Estimates of the rate of growth of expenditure, incomes, and output even at times point in different directions, and their calculated levels can be quite widely apart. In any case, what is a Bank of England official *today* supposed to do in response to the latest quarterly figures of nominal incomes. For example, in October 1990 the latest figures available relate, I think, still only to the first quarter of 1990. Exactly how is a Bank of England official, or are the authorities more generally, supposed to vary the flexible instrument of interest rates on a continuous market on the basis of these occasional (with a large element of erratic error in them) long-past statistics of nominal incomes?

One possible argument is that if one wants to have a workable monetary policy rule along these lines, it may well be better to target inflation alone, rather than set the target in terms of nominal incomes. The data on prices and inflation are somewhat better and more up to date: even so, remember that the Retail Price Index (RPI) statistic includes certain elements which would make its use as a basis for a policy rule quite inappropriate. For example, it responds to mortgage interest rate changes. Varying interest rates in response to an RPI which had itself varied because of a prior movement of interest rates would be an own goal. The RPI also includes indirect taxes and shocks from raw material price changes, such as oil shocks. If a decision was taken to have a strategy, or rule, based on adjusting monetary policy instruments in response to inflation, one would undoubtedly need to derive and devise a quite separate and different form of price index for that purpose. If one did go down this road, one would probably end with a rule indicating that the authorities should change nominal interest rates in relation to the latest change in the specially devised inflation series. The appropriate adjustment would presumably be greater than one for one, in order to ensure that, when inflation went up, real interest rates would rise; consequently nominal interest rates would have to rise faster than the inflation rate. Although this is again theoretically possible, I do not think that it is likely to be adopted.

The reasons for doubting whether such a policy would be acceptable are several. First, if there was such a formula-fixing of interest rates, the authorities would, no doubt, soon want to override their own formula. Consider the possibility of an upward shift in inflation, and hence in interest rates, shortly before an important election. Again this kind of formula would reinforce and re-emphasise the fact that it is the authorities who are changing interest rates. One of the advantages, a great *political* advantage of monetary targets, was that it made interest rates the apparent *market-determined residual* to a decision on monetary aggregates that the authorities were separately taking. So the authorities could then say that it was none of their business that the interest rates had changed. They could claim that they were having to control monetary aggregates, and, given this control, the market had adjusted interest rates by such and such. That was always a fairly thin argument, especially given the way that the authorities operated the techniques of control within the UK, but the formula fixing would make the authorities' hand in changing interest rates even more clearly apparent.

Besides the political disadvantages of this approach, I also have a serious concern about the instabilities that may arise in the use of such instruments, because of long *lags* between changes in interest rates and such changes affecting the economy as a whole. When the authorities observe inflation rising and raise interest rates in response, it takes quite a long time before such interest rate changes affect first the real economy and then the inflation rate (witness the slow reaction in 1989 and 1990 to the increases in interest rates following the worsening inflationary conditions starting in 1988). Consequently if one has some such formula relationship, and inflation stubbornly refuses to go down, month after month, the formula may require repeated sharp increases in interest rates, until ultimately they reach such a high level that the economy then collapses. Then, the slow reaction of the economy to interest rate changes may lead to interest rates being driven down to absurdly low levels in the subsequent depression, if such formula-fixing is maintained.

Instrument instability can occur when one's policy instrument, in this case interest rates, affects the economy with a lag. Let me provide a numerical example. In Case 9.1 below, interest rates have a sizeable effect on incomes immediately in the current period, t, but the effect dies rapidly away, with smaller coefficients at $t-1$ and $t-2$, as time passes.

$$(1) \quad Y_t = 10{,}000 - 700_{rt} - 200_{rt-1} - 100_{rt-2} \qquad \text{(Case 9.1)}$$

$$(2) \quad Y_t = 10{,}000 - 200_{rt} - 600_{rt-1} - 200_{rt-2} \qquad \text{(Case 9.2)}$$

In Case 9.2, the lag profile for interest rate effects on the economy is undoubtedly more realistic, with the main effect not occurring until after a one-period lag. Indeed the lags involved are notoriously long in this respect. Now note that if a decision was made (say on the basis of some long-term forecast) to raise interest rates now by 0.1 per cent and then to hold that new level, then one would get the same ultimate effect on incomes, Y, in both cases, i.e. a fall of 100; the time path will be different, but the end result exactly the same.

If, however, somebody tells the authorities that they must not change interest rates according to their own discretion (and expectation of what is needed not only in the present but in the future), but someone gives them a rule that requires them to change interest rates in such a way as to bring Y down by 100 immediately, and to hold that new level of Y thenceforward (which is the kind of rule that is often advocated), then the outcome, and practicality, of operating differs markedly between Case 9.1 and Case 9.2. In Case 9.1 the change in interest rates necessary to maintain the small constant decline in incomes is very straightforward to introduce. If the effect is immediate, then one can use policy instruments quickly and easily to achieve the desired path for the objective variable. If, however, there are lags in the effect of monetary policy on nominal incomes, then one tends to get such instrument instability.

Let me give a numerical example of the path of interest rates required to reduce Y by 100 in all future periods in the two cases:

As can be seen, with the bulk of the effect coming through instantaneously in Case 9.1, there is only a slight need for interest rates initially to overshoot their long-term equilibrium, in order to achieve the immediate desired reduction in incomes; and thereafter the required path of interest rates rapidly converges to a constant.

The situation is quite different with Case 9.2. Because the effect on Y is initially weaker, one needs a *much* stronger immediate increase to reduce Y sufficiently (0.5 as against 0.14). But when the effect of that sharp rise really does come through after one lag, its effect on Y is then so powerful that it has to be offset by an even larger offsetting contemporaneous change in the opposite direction. As can be seen from the numerical example, this can induce what is known in jargon terms as an 'anti-damped cycle'. Indeed we seemed to observe some such anti-damped cycle when the Federal Reserve Board (Fed) in the

Change in				*Period*		
r	1	2	3	4	5	6
Case 9.1	+0.14	+0.10	+0.09	+0.10	+0.10	+0.10
Case 9.2	+0.50	−1.0	+3.0	−7.5	+20.0	−52.0

USA tried to control their monetary base on a constant quarter-by-quarter basis in the years 1979–82. When such lags between changing the policy instrument and its effect on the economy exist, then trying to control the path of final objectives in a predetermined manner is liable to lead to potentially violent instability in some of those instruments.

9.3   AN EXTERNAL TARGET? EMS, EMU AND GEMU

For all these reasons, I do not believe that withdrawal from monetary targetry is likely to be replaced by an alternative nominal income, or direct inflation, target or rules. The main alternative to such *internal* targetry has always been to adopt an external target. The UK has now taken a step in this direction by joining the European Exchange Rate Mechanism (ERM) of the European Monetary System (EMS). The UK authorities had always insisted that we *would* join the ERM of EMS subject to two conditions having been satisfactorily met. The first was that the UK should have converged to a common EMS country rate of inflation. The second was that British wanted the chance to observe the working of the ERM and to find out if it still works satisfactorily *after* the removal of exchange controls in all the major countries, e.g. France, Italy and possibly Spain: (Luckily the UK did not in the end feel the need to wait until Greece had got rid of its exchange controls). Unfortunately the first condition, that our inflation rate should have converged to the average of our EMS partners, was not met prior to ERM entry but the UK has since been getting closer to it. It is not, however, quite as widely appreciated within the UK that although our inflation rate has for a time been worsening, so has that in many of the major countries in Europe, notably, of course, including Germany.

I want now to confront the argument that the need for convergence in inflation rates (as indeed in other economic developments) has been demonstrated to be less valid, in the context of West German currency reunification with Eastern Germany. Surely, the argument goes, the difference between East Germany and West Germany in all, or virtually all, economic respects is considerably greater than the divergence between West Germany and France and/or the UK. If a united Germany can have a currency reunification, why should the UK have hesitated to join the ERM? Indeed this line of argument has already been adopted with some enthusiasm in Brussels, when an official of the Community was reported in *The Financial Times*, on 8 February 1990, as saying that, 'given the German desire for monetary reunification, he wished to hear no further lectures on the need for convergence from President Pöhl of the Deutsche Bundesbank'. Now my view is that this argument (that has been accepted quite widely) is inherently flawed; indeed it is actually fallacious. In many respects German monetary reunification will be considerably easier (and certainly in many ways more immediately desirable) than monetary unification within Europe as a whole. In fact, the German success is almost guaranteed, largely as a result of West Germany's considerable direct financial support of East Germany and the common monetary policy conducted from Frankfurt by the Bundesbank Central Bank Council even prior to political reunification (see Kloten, 1990).

The key point is that in economies (such as our own in the UK) labour markets tend to work highly imperfectly, with most workers looking over their shoulders at what other workers in other parts of the country are getting, even though the demand/supply conditions for, say, post office workers is totally different in, say, Glasgow than it is in London. The willingness of British workers to accept differential wages in two areas of the same country is limited, despite major differences in local demand/supply conditions. Again the British ambulancemen's union leader, Mr Poole, will be quoting what the firemen received and what the policemen obtained in their own wage bargains; and no doubt, when Mr Poole's ambulancemen get their pay increase, other skilled workers in the medical unions will again look back to what Poole's workers got. If you look at the way that union leaders bargain you will see that the labour markets have a tendency to look backwards: 'I'm not going to get less than he got, and I want as much as so and so', irrespective of local demand and supply conditions. So, in the UK we have a labour market with strong backward-looking relationships.

Backward-looking relationships make it difficult to adjust wage rates in line with local demand/supply conditions (and to expectations of aggregate future inflation) on any very flexible basis. When one considers UK participation in the ERM, say on an irrevocably fixed exchange rate basis, one needs to think of a few relevant numbers. At the moment our rate of growth of productivity in the tradeable goods industries is worse than that in West Germany. Their productivity growth is, maybe, of the order of 3½ to 4 per cent per annum and their growth of wages is such that unit labour costs must normally be expected to rise (ignoring current problems with East Germany) on the order of zero to 1 per cent per annum. Admittedly our own growth of productivity in our tradeable goods industries has *recently* been higher than in West Germany, but that has depended on certain favourable developments; nevertheless let us assume that it remains at about 4 per cent as well. That means that we must get nominal wage rate increases down to around 4 or 5 per cent (and that is being optimistic) if we are to hold irrevocably fixed parities with the DM. But we never achieved anything like that, even in the most favourable conditions in the mid-1980s, favourable in the sense that the slack in the labour market was such that you would have expected wages to have grown very sluggishly, indeed much more slowly than actually then occurred. We never got wage increases down, even then with unemployment of 3 million (13 per cent), to levels that would enable us to maintain a comfortable peg against the DM. What will it take in the way of unemployment, if only for a 'transitional' period, to achieve irrevocably fixed parity with the DM?

But the same should *not* be the case in East Germany because such backward-looking relationships and labour imperfections will, almost by necessity, be absent. The East Germans are now changing their whole economic system, including the whole system of prices and wages, which were previously set within a *command* economy. A completely new system of markets, a whole new system of finance, and of private ownership will shortly be introduced. Under these circumstances, there should be a considerable degree of wage flexibility (without ingrained backward-looking concerns about who else is getting what). One caveat to that, a crucial issue for the success of German currency reunification, must be to try to ensure that East Germans do not look across the border to West Germany, and then immediately attempt to achieve the same real wage rate as in West Germany. That would be the one condition that could make German currency reunification potentially disastrous. If, instead, they can maintain wage flexibility (without the kind of backward-looking nexus that we, in the UK, carry around on our backs all the time), the move to currency reunification should go through a great deal more smoothly (than may well be the case in the run up to European Monetary Union (EMU)).

In addition to such wage flexibility, there are now in Germany a number of other factors which will make currency reunification there a great deal easier, and to some extent, more desirable than within Europe as a whole. First, the degree of mobility of labour and capital will be vastly greater within a reunified Germany, than between the separate countries of Europe. Second, there will soon be a single federal German fiscal system whereby there will be unrequited transfers through the federal tax system to the more depressed Eastern regions. It is precisely when such federal fiscal systems exist to offset the disadvantaged regions (the regions that are getting asymmetric shocks) that a currency union works best. There have been few examples of a successful currency union in areas without a properly-working federal fiscal system (Germany will have it: Europe will not). Finally, of course, there will be a greater degree of social and political cohesion within Germany, than within the whole of Europe, which again will make German monetary reunification much easier to put through successfully than EMU. So unfortunately, the argument that, if the Germans can do it, then why cannot the UK, since we are closer in our economic characteristics to West Germany than are the East Germans, is oversimplified and wrong. It will, alas, be much easier for the Germans to establish currency unification (which I strongly favour), than to achieve the adoption of European monetary unification (which I would still regard as problematical).

9.4 EXCHANGE CONTROLS AND THE 'NEW' EMS

The second qualification over our entry to the ERM had been that the system should have been shown to have been working well, even *after* the abolition of exchange controls. Now some say that that has happened already, that we already observe that the ERM does not need exchange controls to function successfully. Since March 1987 there has only been one realignment, which did not involve any major jump in exchange rates, only a rebasing of the central parity of the Italian lira (in the course of the adoption of the standard narrower (2¼ per cent) bands in January 1990): indeed the earlier (than required) adoption of such narrower bands was in itself a vote of confidence in the continued successful working of the ERM. During this three-year period (1987–90), there has been increasingly less utilisation of exchange controls, as can be observed by the absence of significant differentials between the Euro-lira rates or Euro-franc rates (which are unconstrained) and Italian and French domestic interest rates which potentially could have still been protected by exchange controls. Moreover, Belgium and Luxembourg have meanwhile abandoned their dual exchange rate. France has got rid of its exchange controls, and Italy has gone a long way towards getting rid of its exchange controls.

Many economists, including myself, had argued that the pegged, but adjustable, system of ERM appeared, in its earlier days until 1987, to depend quite heavily on exchange controls. We suggested that, when exchange controls were dropped, there would be a potential danger of speculative attacks overwhelming the countries' attempts to hold their pegs, and that there would be *forced* realignments, and other market perturbations, on occasions when realignment was seen as possible, or *potentially* desirable. Yet it would seem that we have been shown to have been wrong. So some claim that the second qualification has *already* been met. Despite this clear lessening of dependence on exchange controls, the working of the ERM over the last two years, or more, has actually been calm and tranquil. Perhaps the dangers foreseen by some sceptics simply were not there. The hope, and optimistic viewpoint, is that such foreseen problems and pressures did not eventuate because convergence between ERM members has been somewhat greater (than earlier).

Now I do not myself think that that argument has been completely proven. I was most impressed, instead, by a publication by Francesco Giavazzi, who is in my view probably the foremost expert on the EMS, together with Luigi Spaventa (Giavazzi and Spaventa, 1990). I would not wish to plagiarise; in the next section, any *correct* analysis is due to their work.

They have constructed a model which can account for the main stylised facts of recent economic developments in the Southern Cone countries of the EMS, including Italy, Spain and Portugal (and more uncertainly France, for the latter country *has* now converged more closely with West Germany; so the French case is probably better explained by a different model). However, for the rest their model does seem to fit certain recent economic developments quite well.

Anyhow let me set out the key equations:

$$y_t = -\beta r_t + \alpha \lambda_t + \delta f_t \tag{9.1}$$

$$\lambda = e + p^* - p \tag{9.2}$$

$$E(p_{t+1} - p_t) = (p_t - p_{t-1}) + b \ y_t \tag{9.3}$$

$$r_h = i - E(p_{t+1} - p_t) \tag{9.4}$$

$$r_b = \min \begin{cases} i - E(p_{t+1} - p_t) \\ i^* + E(e_{t+1} - e_t) - E(p_{t+1} - p_t) \end{cases} \tag{9.5}$$

Equation 9.1 states that real output depends on the real interest rate, r, that is the nominal interest rate, i, after adjustment for inflationary expectations, $E(p_{t+1} - p_t)$, the real exchange λ, that is the nominal exchange rate, e, after adjustment for price movements at home and abroad, and on fiscal policy, f_t. Equation 9.2 sets out the definition of the real exchange rate, defined in the standard (non-British) manner, so that a higher λ implies a more competitive, more depreciated real exchange rate. So, the coefficient on λ in Equation 9.1 is positive. In Equation 9.3 the determination of inflation is modelled as somewhat backward-looking. Giavazzi and Spaventa then divide the economy into two groups, first households with the majority of their borrowing being done domestically. So, they have to pay the domestic rate of interest, and their real rate obviously then depends upon the prospective internal rate of inflation (Equation 9.4). The second group consists of firms, which can borrow abroad, or they can borrow at home, so that the nominal interest rate that they pay is the minimum of either the domestic interest rate or the foreign interest rate adjusted by their expectation of how their nominal exchange rate will vary against the exchange rate of the other members of EMS, notably West Germany; and the real rate of interest in either case depends on *domestic* inflation (Equation 9.5).

The key point of the Giavazzi and Spaventa paper was that, after 1987, agents began to recognise that it was quite likely that a country within ERM would hold its exchange rate pegged for quite a long period of time, and be able to do so. Accordingly, for short periods of borrowing, the expected probability that the nominal exchange rate would be realigned (depreciated against the DM) had now fallen quite low. If a country joins the ERM, e.g. Spain and Portugal, or establishes a narrow band, Italy, then the first two terms in the second version of Equation 9.5 will be low, i.e. firms in these countries can borrow at West German nominal interest rates, which are much lower than domestic rates. The resulting real rate that firms will pay, assuming that the expectation of no depreciation holds, will be the West German rate less domestic inflation.

So in these years the effective real rate of interest of Italian, Spanish and Portuguese firms (and also possibly to a degree of the French) went down very sharply. The consequence was monetary expansion with large-scale capital inflows, with the exchange rate often appreciating towards the top of its band, causing these countries in practice to have to sterilise massive inflows and build up huge foreign exchange reserves. But because real incomes were thus subject to upwards pressure on joining the ERM (owing to what turned out to be *expansionary* monetary policy), inflation does not go down (Equation 9.3). In fact there is no resultant discipline on the inflation rate. What then occurs is that the real exchange rate continues to appreciate, and the current account balance worsens. That is a plausible picture of what has been happening in the Southern Cone countries. Indeed, there may even be problems of basic stability. In such a system, if the effect on the economy of the real interest rate is greater than the effect on real incomes of the real exchange rate, then the system can explode with inflation ever rising, real interest rates continually falling, and the external position continually worsening. In practice that must eventually become impossible, with the allocation of resources within these countries becoming totally distorted, with resources shifting ever more out of the tradeable goods industries into those sectors, e.g. housing, construction, most susceptible to falling real interest rates.

One implication of this analysis, a point that I have reiterated on quite a few occasions (Goodhart, 1989a, 1989b and 1990), is that the abandonment of the use of monetary policy instruments, within the EMS, for domestic stabilisation purposes requires the *more* flexible and determined use of fiscal policy by nation states for that purpose. Clearly the potential explosive instability of the economy in the case set out above *could* be constrained by sufficiently deflationary fiscal policy, i.e. if fiscal policy was made more deflationary to offset the expansionary effect of capital inflows.

9.5 CENTRAL BANK INDEPENDENCE?

Meanwhile the UK took the plunge and joined the ERM partly because such entry appeared the most widely accepted remedy, in some quarters almost seen as a panacea, for restraining inflation; it is also partly because of internal political dynamics, with the Labour Party having embraced entry into the ERM as one of the key planks in their economic policy, with many of the Conservative Party convinced of the desirability of that same step, and with the then Prime Minister, Mrs Thatcher, though still probably unconvinced of the merits of the case, nevertheless being forced to compromise on the issue.

Nevertheless, for the reasons outlined above, there may still be several difficulties in the operation of the immediate next stage of the EMS, let alone in moving on to the subsequent Stages 2 and 3 of the Delors Committee's Report outline plan. First, to the extent that the adoption of a nominal exchange rate peg is credibly believed to be likely to be successfully maintained, ERM membership could introduce an (inappropriate) monetary stimulus, thereby actually reinforcing inflation for a time. In practice, however, the economic and political circumstances at the time of our entry raised doubts, especially in financial markets, about such commitment. Second, even if contra-inflation discipline is maintained following British entry into the ERM, then the effect of this discipline may fall undesirably on unemployment, rather than on inflation, causing a rise in unemployment and a backlash against the ERM that could have severe political and economic consequences.

So, it would be unwise to regard entry into the ERM, and the establishment of an external anchor, as the final harbour and resting place for monetary policy, beyond which it is unnecessary to look. If, for one reason or another, the decision of the United Kingdom Government to participate in the ERM would be perceived as a failure, what then would happen? I argued earlier that both the readoption of quantitative monetary targets, or the adoption of a nominal income target, were unlikely to be successful. If now an external anchor should also prove to drag, rather than to hold, where then would we turn for some assurance of reasonable price level stability?

There is now, I believe, a possible answer to that question in the concept of the constitutional establishment of an *independent* central bank. This is, indeed, an idea whose time has, almost, come. Such Acts, establishing the independence of their Central Bank, have been passed into law in New Zealand and Chile. Nigel Lawson reported that he had been considering such a step in his speech in the House of Commons, following his resignation in the autumn of 1989 (Lawson, 1989). Sir George Blunden, then the Deputy Governor of the Bank of England, discussed the question of whether the Bank should be made independent in his Julian Hodge lecture in Cardiff in February 1990 (Blunden, 1990). When senior officials of the central bank themselves discuss an issue in public, that once must have seemed to be extremely radical, one must assume that it is a practical possibility, possibly even a probability for future enactment.

The basic idea is that the achievement of price stability is not so much a question of technical feasibility, and of the complexities of economic management, but much more a question of the necessary reorganisation of the fundamental structure of the economic system, so that the natural workings of that system, and the incentives on those in authority, lead towards price stability. The concern has always been that the pressures on a democratically elected government would be to elevate the short-term advantages of expansionary monetary policy above the long-term consequences on inflation. So, the argument goes, one could make the central bank independent of such external (political) pressure; or at least make the imposition of political imperatives on the central bank both more transparent and more (politically) difficult and dangerous for the political authorities.

Meanwhile, the central bank would not be given independence in order to undertake whatever objectives the officials there thought desirable, but, rather, the objective of the achievement of some reasonable measure of price stability would be written into the constitutional Act granting such independence. Moreover, besides being given the legal duty to give price stability priority, the suggestion has often been made, including by myself at times, that the incentive structure should be made even clearer by tying the salary of the most senior officials in the central bank to the outcome that was achieved for inflation over some reasonable length of time. Thus a central bank governor might be given a low *basic* salary; I have often suggested that this might be the equivalent of the salary of a professor of economics; and then, on top of that, the governor might be given a bonus, the amount of which should be calibrated by the closeness with which the system reached price stability after an appropriate length of time, with the amount of that bonus rising to *very high* levels, should the governor manage to deliver price stability (I would think of a bonus of half a million £ per annum for the achievement of price stability).

There are a number of qualifications, and caveats, to this proposal. First, if the central bank is given both the independence and the incentive to achieve price stability, then there are those who fear that it might be tempted to over-do the deflation in the early years, in order to be sure of achieving the *desideratum* of price stability by the deadline established. There are a number of possible responses to this fear. First, it can be argued that the incentives and pressures have all been in the other direction in recent decades, so that it might be salutary to have the incentives on the other side for once. Second, it may be argued that once private agents within the economy see that the incentives really are in the other direction, then they will rapidly revise their own expectations of future inflation, allowing the system to revert to price stability, with less unemployment and disruption than might otherwise occur.

Third, for those who are not persuaded by these arguments, an alternative suggestion, advanced for example by Professor Robert Hall (Hall, 1986), has been to express the objectives for an independent central bank in terms of the deviations both of inflation (or, more toughly, of the price level) from its desired outcome and *also* of the deviation of unemployment (or real incomes) from its desired level. The desired trade-off between the two would determine the weights in the loss function, shown below, that the central banks would be asked to minimise:

$$L = b_1 \, (p - \bar{p})^2 + b_2 \, (u - \bar{u})$$

The other main objection to an independent central bank is that it would give the two main instruments of policy, fiscal and monetary, to two constitutionally separated bodies.

A likely result of this would be that these two major policies would be less well coordinated than heretofore. Again certain objectors have pointed to the difficulties, and disturbances, that have occurred in the world economy as a result of the lack of coordination between fiscal and monetary policy within the USA. While I fully appreciate this crucial problem, it does seem once again to point to the difficulty of analysing, and of politically achieving, the appropriate direction of fiscal policy (once monetary policy is predicated towards the objective of achieving either an external, or internal, anchor for the establishment of price stability, and whether that is in terms of joining the ERM, or of giving the achievement of internal price stability absolute priority). The problem, I feel, lies not so much with the dedication of monetary policy to the prior objective of controlling inflation, but rather with the design of the appropriate fiscal policy in such conditions.

Moreover, on the present plans of the Delors Committee for the future development of the EMS, the European System of Central Banks (ESCB) or Euro-Fed, as it is currently becoming known), would be, itself, entirely independent of the political authorities; indeed, this is a *sine qua non* for the West Germans, and in particular for the Deutsche Bundesbank a necessary precondition of their acceptance of the prospective future stages of the Plan (see Frowen, 1991). As the UK has joined the ERM, we must envisage that, in the subsequent development of the EMS, the Bank of England would therefore have to be granted more independence. But, I have argued above that, if we had failed to join the ERM, the only alternative possible present approach that would provide some guarantee of price stability might also seem to involve the provision of a measure of independence for the Bank of England. So, one way or the other, it looks highly likely that the topic of such independence will be high on the politico-economic agenda for the next few years.

If that, too, should fail to provide an acceptable *modicum* of price stability, then we may be forced to consider ideas that seem even more radical at present, such as reverting to 'free banking'. But to consider the latter now seriously would both be more pessimistic, in the sense that it would involve the assumption that an independent central bank would also fail, and also would involve looking further forward into the future than I think can be justified at the present juncture. So, I would like to leave with a toast: 'best wishes and good luck to the independent central bank of the future'!

References

Blunden, Sir George (1990) Julian Hodge Lecture (Cardiff, February).
Frowen, S. F. (1991) 'A German Perspective of a European Single Market and EMU', in Paul Davidson and J. A. Kregel *Economic Problems of the 1990s* (Edward Elgar Publishing Ltd.).
Giavazzi, F. and Spaventa, L. (1990) 'The "New" EMS', Centre for Economic Policy Research (CEPR) Paper No. 369, (January).
Goodhart, C. A. E. (1989a) 'Delors Report: Was Lawson's Reaction Justifiable?', London School of Economics (LSE) Financial Market Group, Special Paper No. 15; also published in House of Lords Select Committee on the European Communities, 'The Delors Committee Report', HL Paper 3, Session 1989–90, 2nd Report.
Goodhart, C. A. E. (1989b) 'International Financial Linkages' LSE Financial Market Group, Special Paper No. 21 (Conference held by the Federal Reserve Bank of New York, Autumn, published in the conference proceedings, 1991).

Goodhart, C. A. E. (1990) 'Economic and Monetary Union: A British Perspective', LSE Financial Market Group, Special Paper No. 24 (Paper presented at the conference of the Committee of the European Economic Association (CEEA) at their Frankfurt conference, 22–24 February 1990; to appear in the conference proceedings.)

Hall, Robert E. (1986) 'Optimal Monetary Institutions and Policy', Chapter 6 in *Alternative Monetary Regimes*, eds. C. D. Campbell and W. R. Dougan, (Baltimore: Johns Hopkins University Press).

Kloten, Norbert (1990) 'Opportunities and Risks Associated with the Creation of a Uniform Currency Area between the two Germanys', Bank for International Settlements *BIS Review*, no. 104, 29 May, pp. 1–11.

Lawson, Nigel (1989) House of Commons Speech, (October), *Hansard*.

McCallum, B. T. (1987) 'The Case for Rules in the Conduct of Monetary Policy: A Concrete Example', *Federal Reserve Bank of Richmond Review*, Sept./Oct., pp. 10–19.

McCallum, B. T. (1988) 'Robustness Properties of a Rule for Monetary Policy', *Carnegie-Rochester Conference Series on Public Policy*, no. 29, Autumn, pp. 173–203.

Name Index

Name Index

Arestis, P., *14, 80*

Baker, J. A., *58*
Bazdarich, M., *30*
Begg, D., *141*
Blunden, Sir George, 155, *158*
Bockelman, Horst, 40
Brayton, F., *30*
Bruneel, D., *100*
Buscher, H. S., 59, *80*

Campbell, C. D., *159*
Cargill, T., *30*
Chick, Victoria, *80*
Chrystal, K. A., *141*
Coenen, G., xiv
Coes, D. V., *141*
Corden, W. M., *141*
Courakis, A. S., *128*

Darby, M., *30*
Davidson, P., *158*
Dornbusch, R., *141*
Dougan, W. R., *159*

Fischer, S., *141*
Flemming, J. S., viii, **120–8**, 127, *128*
Frenkel J. A., *141*
Friedman, M., *30*
Frowen, Stephen F., viii, *15, 31, 57*, **59–81**, *80*, 158, *158*

Geisler, K.-D., *58*
Giavazzi, Francesco, 152–3, *158*
Goodhart, C. A. E., viii–ix, xii-xiii, *128*, **142–59**, 154, *158–9*
Gurley, R., 28, *30*

Hafer, R., *58*
Hall, Robert, 157, *159*
Hallman, Jeffrey, 25–6, *30*
Hetzel, Robert, *30*
Hodgman, D. R., *141*
Hoover, K., *30*

Jaffee, D. M., 126, *128*
Judd, John, 22, 25, 28, *30*

Kloten, Norbert, ix, xiii, **32–58**, *58, 159*
Köhler, Claus, ix–x, **1–15**, *14–15*
Kregel, J. A., *158*
Krugman, P. R., *141*

Lamont, N., 142
Lawson, Nigel, 142, 143, 155, *159*
Leigh-Pemberton, R. 119, 123, *128*
Lindsey, David, 21, 22, *30*
Lodsey, D., *30*
Lombra, M., *30*

McCallum, B. T., *31*, 143, *159*
MacDonald, R., *141*
Mauskopf, E., *30*
Mayer, Thomas, x, xiii, **16–31**, 18, 23, 28, *31*
McKinnon, R. I., 52, *58, 141*
McNees, Stephen, 24, *31*
Meyer, L., *30*
Meltzer, A. H., 23, *31*, 14, *143*
Miller, M. H., 124, *128*
Miller, Stephen, 22, *31*
Modigliani, F., 23, *31*

Neuman, M. J. M., 59, *81*

161

Osugi, K., *119*

Pepper, Gordon, x–xi, xii-xiii, **129–41**
Pierce, J., 29, *31*
Pöhl, R. O., 149
Poole, Roger, 149
Poole, W., *30*, 143
Porter, Richard, 25–6, *30*

Rasche, R., 18, *30*, *31*
Raymond, Robert, xi, **82–100**
Reichenstein, W., 24, *31*
Rosenblum, H., 17, *31*
Russell, T., 126, *128*

Scadding, J., *30*
Schlomann, Heinrich, xi, *57*, **59–81**, 65, 71, 76, *81*
Schroeder, W., 59, *81*
Shaw, E., 28, *30*
Small, David, 26, *30*

Spaventa, Luigi, 152–3, *158*
Sprenkle, C. M., 124, *128*
Stern, Gary, 19–20, *31*
Stiglitz, J. E., 126, *128*
Storin, S., 17, *31*
Suzuki, Y., *31*, *119*

Tamura, Tatsuya, **101–19**
Thatcher, Margaret, 155
Tobin, J., xiii, 128, *128*
Trehan, Bharat, 22, 25, 28, *30*, *31*

Walsh, Carl, 28, *31*
Weiss, A., 126, *128*
Wenninger, J., 21, *31*
Williamson, J., 58
Wood, G. E., *141*

Yomo, H., *31*

Zarnowitz, Victor, 24, *31*

Subject Index

Baker Plan, 8
Balance of payments, components, 129
Bank of England, independence, 155–6, 158
Bank of Japan
 assessment of money supply movements, 118–19
 control of interbank interest rates, 106–7
 estimates of money supply increase rates, 104
 policy on monetary aggregates, 101–2
Banks, UK
 compared with building societies, 121
 controls on lending, 121
 high interest bearing accounts, 122
 mortgage business growth, 122
 see also Central banks
Basle agreement, 87
Belgium, dual exchange rate, 152
Bond markets
 changes associated with business cycle, 135
 effect on national monetary policies, 10
 expansion, 9–10
 failure of self-regulating mechanisms, 9–10
 foreign investment, 134
 France, 96; blurring of boundaries, 89; bond issues, 86–7; factors attracting investors, 87–8; growth, 85–6; role in economy, 86
 Japan: government issues, 111; yields, 108, 111
 US monetary policy, 18–19
 yields: fluctuations, 10; increased to encourage savings, 134
Borrowing requirement, in French

corporate and public sectors, 83
Budget deficits
 effect on domestic economy, 138
 effect on individual countries, 139
 means of financing, 133–4
Building societies
 compared with banks, 121
 special deposits, 122
Business cycles
 and changes in bond and stockmarkets, 135
 effect of capital flow/exchange rate relationship, 132

CAC 40 index contracts, 94
Capital flows, 1, 14, 154
 and relative monetary growth, 136–7
 causes of movements, 132
 driving exchange rates, 137
 inflow to finance US deficit, 139–40
 influence of return on capital employed, 133
 influence on business cycles, 132
 long-term, 129; reasons for growth in 1980s, 130
 profit expectations, 135
 short-term, behaviour in 1970s, 130
 supply/demand pressures, 135–6
Capital gains, from French bond market, taxation of, 88
Capital markets, France, 84
Capital movement controls, abolition in Europe, 53
Capital transactions neutrality, 14
Central bank money stock
 as main German indicator, 32, 33
 Bundesbank definition, 33
 compared with M3, 34
 disadvantages as target, 37–8

Central bank money stock *cont.*
 forecast growth rate, 35–6
 functions as indicator and target
  variable, 34
 indirect control, 39–41
 monthly calculations, 39–40
 practical application, 41–50
 problems with pinpoint targeting,
  41
 stabilisation, effect on business
  cycle, 49
 target expressed as range, 38–9
 velocity of circulation, 37
Central banks
 and French interbank market, 93
 co-operation, 52; on interest
  rates, 14
 France, interest rate
  management, 98–9
 guidance of exchange rates,
  13–14
 independence, 155–8
 intervention: current account
  imbalances, 131; in foreign
  exchange markets, 131; to
  finance budget deficits, 140
 political influence, 17, 156
 see also Bank of England; Bank
  of Japan; Deutsche
  Bundesbank; Federal
  Reserve
Certificates of deposit
 France, 92
 deregulation in Japan, 112
 in Japanese monetary indicator,
  102, 103
Chile, independence of central
 bank, 155
Chuki-Kokusai fund, 111–12
Commercial paper, French, 92
 effects, 94–5
Commodity prices, 8
Composite Rate Tax, 122
Computers
 and velocity of circulation, 37
 effect on money demand, 114
 resultant financial innovations,
  27, 29
Consumer durables, 124

Corporate sector
 France, borrowing requirement,
  83
 Japan, demand for funds, 103
Council of Economic Experts
 (Germany), 33, 34
Credit
 availability with mortgages, 125
 decline of direct controls, 98
 domestic, changes in UK since
  1979, 120
 effect of interest rates on bank
  lending, 107, 108
 offshore banking facilities, 7
Current account
 affecting interest rate changes,
  129
 and speculators' behaviour, 130
 balances, 5–6; limits, 5
 imbalances, influence on capital
  flows, 131
Cyclical targets, 51

Debt, 6–9, 111
 Baker Plan for sustained growth,
  8
 source of problems, 6–7
Delors Committee, 155, 157–8
Demand, adjustment to potential
 supply, 12–13
Demand for Money, *see* Money
 Demand
Deutsche Bundesbank, 149, 158
 calculation of monetary targets,
  55
 changes after Bretton Woods
  collapse, 32–3
 control of money aggregates in
  mid-1980s, 44
 future policy role, 50–4
 measures adopted in 1987, 45
 monetary policy since 1988, 32,
  55–7
 money stock, strategy since 1988,
  55–7
Deutsche Mark (DM)
 effect of German unification, 79
 exchange rate against US dollar,
  42–3; effect of fluctuations, 3;

in model of demand for
money, 60, 61
sterling exchange rate, 150
Developing countries
Baker plan, 8
current account deficits, 6
use of exchange rate as policy
instrument, 5
Disintermediation
and higher interbank interest
rates, 107, 108
France, 94–6
Japan, 111
Dollar, *see* US dollar

Economic growth
adjusting demand to potential
supply, 12–13
Baker Plan, 8
effect of free floating exchange
rates, 3–4
Germany, in mid-1980s, 42–3
non-inflationary, strategy
implications, 12–13
rates, compared with
unemployment rates, 1
Economic policies
affected by multiple factors,
10–12
international interdependence, 1
national objectives, 1–2
strategy, 12–14
ECU, *see* European Currency Unit
EMS, *see* European Monetary
System
Equity market, French
blurring of boundaries, 89
creation of 'second market', 85
expansion, 84–5
increased demand, 85
ERM, *see* European Exchange
Rate Mechanism
Eurocards, 37
Eurocheques, 37
Eurocurrency markets, 129
European Currency Unit (ECU),
54
European Exchange Rate
Mechanism (ERM), 143, 148

after removal of exchange
controls, 148, 151–4
and model of EMS members'
development, 152–4
UK entry. 148–9, 154–5
European Monetary System
(EMS), 2, 99
aims for 1992, 53
crisis (1986), 44–5
effect of abandoning monetary
policy instruments, 154
effect of inflation rate changes, 3
intervention mechanism, 2; effect
on Bundesbank (1986), 45
realignment (1987), 152
role in economic policy strategy,
12
West German relations with, 53,
54
European System of Central
Banks, 158
Euro-yen assets, 118
Excess reserves, and German
money supply policy, 39, 40
Exchange controls, abolition, 120
and working of ERM, 148, 151–4
Exchange rates, 2–4
and devalued currencies, 4
and money supply targets in
France, 99
central bank guidance, 13–14
central bank market intervention,
131
changes: causes, 129–30; effects,
5; wealth effects, 126, 127
determined by interest rate
differentials, 11
effect on market of economic
news, 138–9
effects on enterprises and
speculators, 4
floating: and internationalisation
of markets, 113; effects, 3
in model of Germany's demand
for money, 61
in nominal money demand
function, 68, 71, 76
interventions, 13
stability, 51–2

Exchange rates, *cont.*
  sterling/DM rates, 150
  targets, 51, 52
  used by heavily indebted
    countries, 5
  volatility, effect on Japanese
    economy, 109
  see also European Exchange
    Rate Mechanism
Exports, from debtor countries

Federal Open Market Committee,
    16–17, 19
Federal Reserve
  and future targeting, 29
  changes in monetary policy
    (1982), 18–23
  effect of interest elasticity on
    money supply control, 21
  effects of interest rate targeting,
    23
  effect of intervention on budget
    deficit, 140
  inability to control M2 or M3, 26
  money targets and information
    variables, 19–20
  protection from political
    pressures, 25
  quarterly control of monetary
    base, 148
  quasi-monetarist policy, 16–18
Financial futures market, France,
    93–4
Financial innovations, 120–8
  and US inflation rate, 27
  categories, 120
  France: effects, 96; role of
    authorities, 83–4
  Germany, 78
  Japan, effects, 114
Financial markets
  and monetary co-operation, 53
  France, expansion, 84
  integration within EMS, 53
  interdependence, 2
  internationalisation, 113; effects,
    50, 95
  Japan, structural changes, 111–14
  liberalisation, effects on

  monetary policy, 125–8
Fiscal policy
  and central bank independence,
    157
  linked to monetary policy, 2
  permissive, effect on capital
    flows, 134
Fisher effect, 24
Fixed interest rate tenders, 46, 47,
    49
FOMC, *see* Federal Open Market
    Committee
Forward exchange rate, in nominal
    money demand function, 62,
    68, 71, 76
France
  decline in credit controls, 98
  disintermediation, 94–6
  dismantling exchange controls,
    95–6, 152
  economy, intermediated financial
    ratio, 96
  financial market development,
    84–94
  role of central bank and
    securities markets, 82
  structure of sectoral surpluses
    and deficits, 83–4
Free markets, 1–2

Germany
  current account surplus, 5, 6
  dependence on foreign money
    markets, 59
  effects on unification, 79–80
  future economic prospects, 50–4
  inflation rate, 149
  model of money demand, 59–80
  money stock as main indicator,
    32, 33
  productivity, compared with UK,
    149–50
  unification of currency, 148–9,
    150–1
  see also Deutsche Bundesbank
Gilt-edged market, effect of
    inflation changes, 138
Globalisation of markets, 50
Gross domestic product (GDP),

effect of budget deficits, 139
Gross national product (GNP)
  as target, 24
  compared with nominal
    production potential, 36
  in nominal money demand
    functions, 62, 65, 68, 71
  Japan, pre- and post-1975, 109,
    110
  problems of accurate forcasting,
    24
  relationship with medium of
    exchange, 26

House price increases, 123–4
Household sector, French, 96
  borrowing requirement, 83

IMF, *see* International Monetary
  Fund
Income, aggregate, 60, 61
Incomes policies, 2
Indicators, adopted at Tokyo
  Summit, 51–2
Inflation
  and UK entry to ERM, 148–9,
    154–5
  as monetary policy rule, 145
  effect on capital flows, 132
  effect on EMS, 3
  Germany, negative rate. 43
  Japan, 109
  reduction, 1
  re-establishment in UK, 142
  US: policy causes, 17; resultant
    financial innovations, 27
Information variables, in US
  monetary targets, 20
Interbank market, 93
Interest rates
  and offshore banking facilities, 7
  as instrument of monetary policy,
    98–9
  changes: according to a formula,
    145–6; effects on individuals
    and corporations, 107; effects
    on private expenditure, 108–9;
    Germany, 46–8; impact on
    expenditure, 126–7; lags before

effects revealed, 146–8; related
    to monetary policy
    effectiveness, 102
  comparability of bank and
    building society deposits, 122
  countering undesirable trends, 49
  differentials determining
    exchange rates, 11
  effect on housing market, 126
  elasticity: and M1 targeting, 28;
    effect on control of money
    supply, 21, 22
  flexibility, time deposits, 21
  French bond market, 87
  hedging against short-term
    changes, 126
  indirect control of central bank
    money stock, 39
  indirect control of funds rate, 119
  interbank, money supply
    management instrument, 106–9
  international monetary markets,
    and debt problem, 8
  Japan, 117: deregulation, 117–18
  on UK mortgages, 121–2
  specification by central banks, 40
  targets, 51
  tenders, 46, 47
  US: achieving stability, 18;
    fluctuation, 16–18; targeting,
    23; to control M2 or M3, 26–7
  variable, influencing demand for
    money, 60, 61
International division of labour, 1
International Monetary Fund
  (IMF), 51
Investment, global diversification,
  127
IS curve, 17, 18
Italy
  decline of credit controls, 98
  EMS realignment (1987), 152
  exchange control abolition, 152
  interest rates, 152–4

Japan
  current account surplus, 5, 6
  decline of credit ceilings, 98
  economic performance

Japan *cont.*
(post-1975), 109–11
financial deregulation measures, 112–13
management of monetary aggregates, 101–11
structural changes in financial markets, 111–14
surplus savings, 135
see also Bank of Japan

Kokusai fund, 112

Labour market imperfections, 149–50
Lagged reserve requirement, 18
Life assurance, 124
Liquidity
demand, 124
German policy, 49
indirect control of central bank money stock, 39
interbank and central bank balances, 39
trap, 43
LM curve, 18
Lombard loans, 39, 41
Lombard rate, 40, 45
Luxembourg, dual exchange rate, 152

M0, 143
M1, 97
compared with central bank money stock, 34
Federal Reserve abandonment of targets, 21–2, 23–5
in model of Germany's demand for money, 60, 61, 78; regressions, 62–5; stability of regressions, 71–8
Japan, 116; limitations as indicator, 103
velocity: including interest-paying transactions accounts, 28; inherent instability, 27–8
M2
compared with central bank money stock, 34
in model of Germany's demand

for money, 60, 61; regressions, 65–8; stability of regressions, 71–8
Japan, 101, 102, 116
use as monetary target, 25–7
velocities, 29
M2 + CDs (Japanese indicator), 103–6, 118–19
M2R, 97
M3
compared with central bank money stock, 34
German 1988–9 targets, 56–7
in model of Germany's demand for money, 60, 61, 78; regressions, 68–71; stability of regressions, 71–8
use as monetary target, 25–7
velocities, 29
M3R, 97
MATIF (*Marché à terme international de France*), 84, 93–4
Minimum interest rate tenders, 47
Minimum reserve obligation, 40
Monetary policy
abandoning use of instruments within EMS, 154
and central bank independence, 157
and price stability, 10–12
co-operation, 53
effect of bond market, 10
effect of debt problem, 8–9
effect of financial market liberalisation, 125–8
effect of structural break in money stock definitions, 71
France, 96–9; change in instruments, 98–9; influence of exchange rates, 99; redefinition of aggregates. 97
Germany: Central Bank Council decisions, 46; Deutsche Bundesbank role, 32; flexibility of instruments, 46; increasing efficiency, 50; since 1988, 55–7
in open world economy, 2
Japan, 101; changes in transmission mechanism, 117;

implications of structural
changes, 114–17
need for coherent strategy, 142–3
problems of instrument
instability, 146–8
role in economic strategy, 13
trustworthiness, 49–50
US: effects of financial
innovations, 21–2, 27; Federal
Reserve role (1979–82), 16–18;
future possibilities, 27–9
Monetary system, freedom from
disruptions, 13
Money demand
Germany, 59–81; factors causing
uncertainty, 78; partial
adjustment model, 61;
short-run analysis, 61;
significant variables, 60, 61;
specification of functions,
62–71; summary of analysis,
78–80
Japan, effect of structural
changes, 114, 116
Money markets
interest rates, in nominal money
demand function, 62, 65, 68
internationalisation, 78
Money movements, 1, 14
see also Capital flows
Money stock
definitions, 59, 76
tripartite control system, 52
see also Central bank money
stock
Money supply
and capital flows, 136–7
influence of interbank interest
rates, 107–9
Japan: central bank assessment
of growth, 118–19;
determination of intermediate
objectives, 104–6; instruments
of management, 106–9; periods
of control, 104; policy, 101–3;
slowdown in growth, 109;
targeting, 103–6
problems of defining indicators,
116–17
targets, 143; based on velocity

estimates, 143–4; derivation,
33–9; external, 148–51;
external influences, 42;
nominal income targets, 144–8;
strategy of Bundesbank, 32–3;
variables, 51
UK, effect of changes in
bank/building society
operations, 123
US: demise of targeting, 21–2,
23–5; effect of interest
elasticity, 21, 22; instability of
M1 velocity, 21, 22, 24;
targets, 19–20, 23, 25–7;
variance in growth rate, 18
Mortgage market, 121
and increasing equity in homes,
123
France, 89
UK: interest rates, 121–2,
rationing, 122; with personal
overdraft facilities, 125

New Zealand, independence of
central bank, 155
Nominal income targets, 114–8, 155
problems of dated statistics, 145
Nominal production potential, 36
Notes of special financial bodies,
92–3
NOW (negotiable order of
withdrawal) accounts, 21

Offshore banking, 7
Oil price shocks, 78, 102, 109, 111,
130, 145
Opportunity cost variables, 79–80
Opportunity costs, 61, 77, 78
Options contracts on notional
loans, 94

Pension funds, 124
Personal sector
additional borrowing, 123
expansion, 124
liquidity, 124–5
types of investment, 124
PIBOR contracts, 94
Political pressures on central banks,
17, 156

Portugal, interest rates, 152–4
Price index, in nominal money
    demand function, 62
  see also Retail Price Index
Prices
  as monetary policy rule, 145
  changes, and central bank money
    stock, 49
  effect of money supply policies,
    10–12
  in model of Germany's demand
    for money, 61
  increases, and money stock
    control, 36
  Japanese inflation, 103
  stability: as goal of policy, 32;
    maintaining, 13; objective of
    independent central banks, 156
Production potential, 55
Productivity growth rates,
    comparative, 149–50
Protectionism, 2
Public sector
  France: and financial innovation,
    84; borrowing requirement, 83
  Japan, demand for funds, 103

Quantity theory, 26

Recession, and monetary targeting,
    36
Rediscounting, 41, 45
Regulation Q (US), 21, 22
  resultant financial innovations, 27
Repurchase agreements, 40–1, 45,
    46–7, 93, 109
Retail Price Index, 145
Return on capital employed,
    influence of capital flows, 133
Rikin fund, 112

Savings
  effects of sudden declines, 134
  financing budget deficits, 134
Securities market
  France, 82–4; characteristics, 89,
    90–1; short-term negotiable
    securities, 89–93
  globalisation, 129

negotiable, 93
  see also Repurchase agreements;
    Unlisted securities market
SICAVs (*sociétés d'investissement à
    capital variable*), 88, 89, 93
Spain, interest rates, 152–4
Spread banking, 117

Taxation, French bond market,
    87–8
Tokyo Economic Summit, 52
Trade deficit, US, effect on rest of
    world, 139–41
Trade imbalances, 137
Trade neutrality, 13, 14
Treasury bills, French, 93
  effect of disintermediation, 95
  negotiable, 92

Unborrowed reserves, US
    monetary policy, 18–19
Unemployment, 155
  rates, 1
United Kingdom
  banks and building societies
    compared, 121
  current account deterioration in
    1974, 130
  ERM entry, 148–9, 155
  lack on monetary strategy, 142–3
  policy changes since 1979, 120
  productivity, compared with
    Germany, 149–150
  see also Bank of England; Banks,
    UK; Building societies
United States
  budget deficit, effect of increase,
    140–1
  capital flows and current account
    imbalances, 130
  current account deficits, 5–6
  low savings level, 136
  recession, 21–2
  trade deficit: effect of increase,
    140; impact, 139–41
  see also Federal Reserve
Unlisted securities market, 85
US dollar
  depreciation, 4; reduction of

current account balances, 4
exchange rate against DM, 42–3;
    fluctuations, 3; in model of
    demand for money, 60, 61

Velocity of circulation, 55, 143–4
central bank money stock, 37

Wage rates, 149–50
West Germany, *see* Germany
Wealth, volume, influence on
    demand for money, 60
World trade volume, and debt
    problem, 8